OXFORD
INDIA SHORT
INTRODUCTIONS

PARTY SYSTEM
IN INDIA

The Oxford India Short
Introductions are concise,
stimulating, and accessible guides
to different aspects of India.
Combining authoritative analysis,
new ideas, and diverse perspectives,
they discuss subjects which are
topical yet enduring, as also
emerging areas of study and debate.

OTHER TITLES IN THE SERIES

For more information, visit our website:
https://india.oup.com/content/series/o/
oxford-india-short-introductions/

OXFORD
INDIA SHORT
INTRODUCTIONS

PARTY SYSTEM
IN INDIA

REKHA DIWAKAR

OXFORD
UNIVERSITY PRESS

OXFORD
UNIVERSITY PRESS

Oxford University Press is a department of the University of Oxford.
It furthers the University's objective of excellence in research, scholarship,
and education by publishing worldwide. Oxford is a registered trademark of
Oxford University Press in the UK and in certain other countries.

Published in India by
Oxford University Press
2/11 Ground Floor, Ansari Road, Daryaganj, New Delhi 110 002, India

ISBN-13: 978-0-19-947959-7
ISBN-10: 0-19-947959-3

Typeset in 11/14.3 Bembo Std
by Excellent Laser Typesetters, Pitampura, Delhi 110 034
Printed in India by Replika Press Pvt. Ltd

Contents

Contents

Tables and Figures

Tables

Figures

Acknowledgements

Writing this book has been both an intellectual delight and a challenge, and I have benefitted immensely from the insightful comments of the two anonymous reviewers, for which I am extremely grateful.

My gratitude goes out to my current and former students, who have always been a source of thought-provoking ideas and queries. I am thankful to the team at Oxford University Press for supporting my book proposal and helping me to keep the project on track.

The research leave granted by the Department of Politics at the University of Sussex, United Kingdom, allowed me to complete the manuscript within the planned time, and is gratefully acknowledged. This project would have been impossible without the support and patience of my family.

Abbreviations

AAP	Aam Aadmi Party
AGP	Asom Gana Parishad
AIADMK	All India Anna Dravida Munnetra Kazhagam
AITC	All India Trinamool Congress
BJD	Biju Janata Dal
BJP	Bharatiya Janata Party
BJS	Bharatiya Jana Sangh
BKD	Bharatiya Kranti Dal
BLD	Bharatiya Lok Dal
BSP	Bahujan Samaj Party
CFD	Congress for Democracy
CMP	Common Minimum Programme
CPI	Communist Party of India
CPM	Communist Party of India (Marxist)
EEP	Encompassing Ethnic Parties

ENP	Effective Number of Parties
DMK	Dravida Munnetra Kazhagam
ECI	Election Commission of India
IAC	India Against Corruption
JD	Janata Dal
JDS	Janata Dal (Secular)
JDU	Janata Dal (United)
JKNC	Jammu and Kashmir National Conference or National Conference
JMM	Jharkhand Mukti Morcha
KLP	Krishikar Lok Party
KMPP	Kisan Mazdoor Praja Party
LDF	Left Democratic Front
LJP	Lok Janshakti Party
MP	Member of Parliament
NCP	Nationalist Congress Party
NEP	Narrow Ethnic Parties
NDA	National Democratic Alliance
NF	National Front
OBC	Other Backward Classes
PDP	Jammu and Kashmir Peoples Democratic Party
PMK	Pattali Makkal Katchi
PR	Proportional Representation (electoral system)
PSP	Praja Socialist Party
RJD	Rashtriya Janata Dal

RSS	Rashtriya Swayamsevak Sangh
SAD	Shiromani Akali Dal
SC	Scheduled Caste
SHS	Shiv Sena
SMPS	Single-member Plurality Electoral System
SP	Samajwadi Party
SSP	Samyukta Socialist Party
ST	Scheduled Tribe
STV	Single Transferable Vote (electoral system)
TDP	Telugu Desam Party
TRS	Telangana Rashtra Samithi
UDF	United Democratic Front
UF	United Front
UPA	United Progressive Alliance
VHP	Vishwa Hindu Parishad
YSRCP	YSR Congress Party

Introduction

At the time of India's Independence in 1947, few expected it to survive as a democracy due to widespread poverty and illiteracy, and the presence of a highly ethnically and linguistically diverse population. However, India has survived as a functioning democracy with a vibrant party system, and, so far, has successfully held 16 national (parliamentary) elections and over 350 state assembly elections to elect its central and state governments. Political parties have played a crucial role in the promotion and sustenance of India's democracy, and remain an important link between the state and the citizens. This book provides an analysis of the nature of the Indian party system since the formation of its oldest party, the Indian National Congress (or Congress), during British colonial rule. Its aim is to acquaint the reader with the characteristics, determinants, and the evolution of the Indian party system given the country's social diversity, and historical and institutional context.

Parties are the key building blocks of a political system, and provide a coordinating mechanism between voters, candidates, legislators, ministers, and other key actors in a polity. They help in strengthening democratic politics and train candidates to contest elections under a party label. Parties engage in electoral competition to win the support of the electorate. A party system consists of competitive interaction amongst parties, and the patterns of their coexistence. The party system works within the country's political, institutional, and social context, and can produce legislative majorities leading to a one-party government or, alternatively, multiparty coalitions. Party systems have important political, social, and economic consequences in a polity. A study of the factors that explain the nature, size, and evolution of the party system can therefore help decipher the social, economic, and political outcomes in a polity.

Key (1964) notes that parties play three core roles in a political system: 'party-in-the-electorate' providing informational shortcuts to the electorate and acting as the party of campaign; 'party-in-government' organizing and coordinating legislative mechanisms, and 'party-as-organization' aggregating and representing public opinion and negotiating between the citizens and the government. Parties vary in terms of size, ideology, and the strategies they adopt to appeal to the electorate. For example, Left-wing parties believe in more state intervention, while Right-wing parties favour a limited role of the state in the provision of public goods and services. Parties that are centrist in their ideology tend to follow more liberal policies. Parties can be elitist with a narrow support base, mass-based that cater to a wide section of the electorate, or 'catch-all' which try to appeal to an even wider section of the voters, cutting across various social cleavages. In a single-party system such as China, party membership provides exclusive benefits to its members. In a two-party system such as the United States, parties tend to be ideologically inclusive and the success of a third party is extremely difficult. In fragmented party systems such as Germany and contemporary India, parties often need to forge alliances with each other and form coalition governments.

Modern parties, of the kind we see today, emerged in the nineteenth century following the expansion of suffrage in Western democracies such as Britain, France, and the United States. In India, the political parties that were first established at the end of the nineteenth and the beginning of the twentieth centuries had a key link with the growth and direction of the country's struggle for independence against British colonial rule. Parties and party systems are shaped by various sociological, institutional, and contextual factors. Lipset and Rokkan (1967) proposed that parties emerge due to the presence of social cleavages, and the need to cater to the interests of different sections of the society. Party formation and survival are also linked to institutional rules, for example, the method of conversion of votes into seats under a given electoral system. Duverger (1963 [1954]) formulated propositions, according to which a single-member plurality electoral system (SMPS) is likely to lead to a two-party system, while multi-member proportional representation electoral system (PR) favours a multiparty system. Party systems are also determined by contextual factors such as the nature of the relationship between the national and state governments, and the temporal, opportunistic incentives of political leaders to form new parties and alliances to gain power.

In multicultural and federal democracies, parties tend to represent diverse interests, and may need to engage in coalition building at the national and the state levels. Spatial models of issue voting have been developed to explain how the ideological positions of parties and voters shape the nature of electoral competition in a polity. While the proximity model predicts that parties tend to converge towards the position of the median voter and adopt a moderate position on issues, the directional model assumes that parties gain by propagating intense views and adopting more radical policies (Hindmoor 2006).

What is the role of political parties in Indian democracy, how has the Indian party system evolved over time, which factors have shaped it, and what are the emerging trends and challenges? These interrelated questions are explored in this book, taking a chronological as well as a thematic approach. The central argument of the book is that the Indian party system has been, and continues to be, shaped by a complex interaction of various sociological, institutional, and contextual factors. In particular, it highlights that India's federal structure, electoral system and rules, as well as the presence of numerous overlapping social cleavages produce an environment of constant flux for the parties.

Chapter 1 provides a background to the Indian party system, including the institutional framework within which it functions, and the typology of parties and party systems in the Indian context. It also summarizes the main lines of research on party systems, and how they relate to the Indian party system.

Chapters 2 to 4 include an analysis of the evolution of the Indian party system, which has gone through a number of phases: Congress's dominance, followed by its decline and the rise of opposition parties, and finally the fragmentation of the party system, emergence of regional parties, and coalition politics. The focus of these chapters is to delineate and unfold various factors, which have shaped the nature of the Indian party system during these phases. Chapter 2 provides an insight into the role of Congress and the nature of party politics during the pre-Independence period and also explains how Congress functioned as an ideal-type broad-based 'system' during the first two decades after India's Independence in 1947. It also analyses the factors that led to the decline of Congress in the 1970s and 1980s, and, in particular, highlights the various institutional and contextual factors that influenced the nature of the party system in India during this period.

The late 1980s and 1990s witnessed the fragmentation of the Indian party system, and the seven national elections held between 1989 and 2009 produced either a minority or coalition government at the centre. This phase also saw the emergence of the Hindu nationalist Bharatiya Janata Party (BJP) as the main challenger to Congress at the national level and in many states, as well as the rise of regional parties, many of which appealed to the voters on the basis of social cleavages of caste and region. Chapter 3 analyses the factors behind the rise of Hindu nationalism, and the BJP in the 1980s, 1990s, and beyond. Chapter 4 explains the main reasons for the fragmentation of the Indian party system in the post–1989 period. It also focuses on the rise of the regional parties, identity politics, and the onset of an era of coalition governments in India beginning in 1989.

Chapter 5 identifies and outlines the emerging trends in the Indian party system following the 2014 national election, in which the BJP was able to win a majority of seats after many years of hung parliaments and coalition governments. This chapter also provides an analysis of the prospects of major political parties in India and presents a prognosis about the evolution of the Indian party system in light of the 2014 national election and the subsequent state assembly elections.

Finally, some overarching conclusions on the key issues and challenges facing parties and party system in India are presented.

1

Parties and Party System in India

Political parties and organizations first emerged in India during the British colonial rule under the influence of Western political ideas. However, they acquired characteristics of their own and can be viewed as a product of historical evolution, rather than merely being a foreign import. The rising political consciousness of the masses during India's Independence movement against the colonial rule led to the establishment of a variety of political parties which, in turn, shaped the framework of the Indian party system post decolonization. In particular, the experience gained by the parties in mobilizing people during India's independence movement was instrumental in their growth and functioning after Independence, which contributed towards the establishment of a democratic political culture in India.

Institutional Framework

India attained independence on 15 August 1947 and adopted its Constitution on 26 January 1950. According to the Constitution, India is a sovereign, socialist, secular, democratic republic and is a union of states with a parliamentary form of government led by a prime minister. Parties in India function within the institutional framework of a federal structure and are bound by the country's electoral laws and rules. The Indian political system is broadly based on UK's Westminster model with two houses of the national parliament: the Lok Sabha, the lower house; and the Rajya Sabha, the upper house. The Lok Sabha is the main legislative body comprising 543 members directly elected from single-member constituencies based on a plurality of votes (SMPS) and 2 nominated members. Elections to the Lok Sabha are held every five years, or earlier if it is dissolved under specific circumstances. Currently, there are 245 members of the Rajya Sabha, of which 12 are nominated by the president of India and 233 are indirectly elected by the members of the state assemblies based on the single transferable vote (STV) system, a type of PR. The president of India is the symbolic head of the state, and is elected indirectly by an electoral college comprising elected members of both the houses of Parliament and state assemblies.

The political setup in the states broadly mirrors the structure at the centre, with an elected state assembly, the Vidhan Sabha, with a chief minister as head of government, and a governor appointed by the central government.

The Election Commission of India (ECI), a constitutional body, is entrusted with the task of registering political parties, allotting party symbols, and planning and conducting elections. It registers parties as national, state, and unrecognized parties based on their performance in elections. Many independent candidates (without a party affiliation) also contest elections in India, but most of them have been unsuccessful in the recent elections. A national party is defined as one that wins seats in at least four states, and its party symbol cannot be used by other parties anywhere in India. Parties that have received a certain proportion of votes or seats in a state can be recognized as a state party. Recognition as a national or a state party gives a party the opportunity to reserve a particular symbol nationally or in the concerned states. Given the large proportion of uneducated voters in India, party symbols assume a greater significance, since these provide a unique visual identity to parties.

A total of 464 parties participated in the latest 2014 national election, of which there were 6 national, 39 state, and 419 registered unrecognized parties.

The number of parties participating in elections has risen since India's first national election in 1952. This increase, especially since the 1990s, has occurred due to the increase in the number of state and registered unrecognized parties, while the number of national parties has remained relatively stable. Further, a higher number of parties have been able to win a significant share of votes and gain representation in the Lok Sabha, as is shown in Table 1.1. The voter turnout has also continued to rise and stood at 66 per cent in 2014, the highest ever in an Indian national election, indicating trust in the electoral process, and more generally in the Indian democracy.

The Need for and Emergence of Parties

An important theme of research on party systems concerns the need for political parties in a democracy. A dominant view within this strand of research explains the need for parties in terms of the self-interested behaviour of voters, candidates, and legislators. For example, voters elect candidates who will best represent and serve their interests, candidates join parties in order to achieve their personal goals, and legislators engage in opportunistic politics, splitting an existing party or joining another, when it serves their objectives. As Aldrich (1995: 186) comments, 'there are more or

TABLE 1.1 Number of Parties in National Elections (Lok Sabha), 1952–2014

Year	Total number of contesting parties[1]	Number of recognized parties[2]			Number of registered unrecognized parties	Number of seat-winning parties	Voter turnout (%)
		National	State	Total			
1952	53	14	39	53	–	22	61
1957	15	4	11	15	–	12	62
1962	27	6	11	17	10	20	55
1967	25	7	14	21	4	18	61
1971	53	8	17	25	28	24	55
1977	34	5	15	20	14	18	60
1980	36	6	19	25	11	17	57
1984	33	7	17	24	9	21	64
1989	113	8	20	28	85	24	62
1991	145	9	27	36	109	24	57
1996	209	8	30	38	171	28	58
1998	176	7	30	37	139	39	62
1999	169	7	40	47	122	38	60
2004	230	6	36	42	188	38	58
2009	363	7	34	41	322	37	58
2014	464	6	39	45	419	38	66

Source: Collated by the author based on ECI election statistics.

Notes: 1. These do not include independent candidates; 2. There were 14 recognized parties on all-India basis during the 1952 election. In the 1957 election, four parties were recognized as national parties.

less continual incentives for ambitious politicians to consider party organizations as means to achieve their goals'.

Thus, to be useful, parties must offer equilibrium solutions to collective dilemmas, which are inherent in democratic politics, and therefore entrepreneurial politicians have strong incentives to set up parties as being long-term commitment devices (Chhibber and Kollman 2004: 14). In this context, parties are seen to solve the 'collective action problem' by aggregating the interests of voters and providing solutions that other institutional arrangements cannot offer. Hence, strong institutionalized parties are seen to be vital for healthy democracies, and a stable party system allows effective government, and provides voters with a clear, predictable, and simplified set of electoral alternatives (Wilkinson 2015). Parties are also viewed as a means to strengthen the functioning of legislatures and are expected to provide stability, especially in the context of coalition politics. They also provide training in party and electoral politics to candidates and party workers.

According to Lipset and Rokkan (1967), political parties emerge due to the existence of social cleavages in a polity, while Taagepera and Shugart (1989) stress that party formation and survival are linked to electoral rules as well as how parliamentary seats are distributed and decided. Parties also emerge due to the advent of new issue dimensions such as immigration, economic reforms, corruption, or environmental concerns, and in general, when voters are dissatisfied with existing parties.

Emergence of Political Parties in India before Independence

Political organizations that represented the interests of the landholders and the new urban middle class were established even before the introduction of the limited electoral process during the British rule. The main objective of these organizations was to achieve greater opportunities for Indians in government jobs and membership of public bodies. The Congress was the most important of these organizations and mainly represented the interests of the middle classes. Formed in 1885, it was essentially India's first political party and represented a range of views, ideologies, and interests. While the moderates or the liberals within the party were more upper middle class and committed to social reforms, the radicals were less committed to constitutionalism and mainly represented the lower middle classes (Weiner 2006). With the introduction of provincial elections by the British in 1919, the Congress gradually transformed into a mass movement, with the main goal to achieve India's Independence.

7

While Congress was the most influential political party during this period, there were also other parties that emerged to represent the interests of specific religious or social groups. The Muslim League, which was formed in 1906 and largely represented the landed aristocracy, aimed at safeguarding the rights of the Muslims. Later, it demanded the creation of a separate nation for Muslims. The formation of the Muslim League and the British government's proposal in 1906 to introduce separate Muslim electorates for the legislative councils prompted the formation of Hindu *sabha*s, or associations/councils, in many Indian provinces to protect the interests of the Hindus.

These Hindu sabhas came together in 1915 to establish an all-India political organization, the Hindu Mahasabha, which became a full-fledged political party in the late 1930s under the leadership of V.D. Savarkar. The Hindu Mahasabha opposed the Muslim League as well as Congress's idea of secular nationalism, but did not receive much electoral support, even as Rashtriya Swayamsevak Sangh (RSS) or National Volunteer Corps, a Hindu cultural organization formed in 1925, continued to promote Hindu culture and nationalist ideology. The Shiromani Akali Dal (SAD) was another religion-based party, which originated from a political movement of the Sikhs in the Punjab province, with the aim of gaining popular control of the Sikh gurdwaras (shrines). Formed in 1920, it became a political force fighting for the rights of the Sikhs in Punjab, especially after India's Independence in 1947.

The colonial phase also witnessed the emergence of other parties based on ideology, ethnic or regional identity, which participated in political activities including seeking representation to the provincial governments. The Communist Party of India (CPI) was formed in 1925 following a conference of various communist groups active in India. It was born out of a fusion of militant, anti-imperialist patriotism with internationalism, the struggle for national liberation, and the class struggle for socialism (CPI website). The CPI sought to represent the interests of Indian workers, and opposed the Congress as well as the British government, who were considered by the party to be part of a capitalist vision of the society. However, it remained relatively indifferent to electoral politics and was active mainly in the urban regions of the country. In the southern parts of India, there were political movements such as the Dravida movement, which challenged the domination of administrative and educational institutions as well as India's Independence movement by Brahmins, who represented the top layer within the traditional hierarchy of caste system amongst Hindus in India. In particular, this movement demanded the de-Brahmanization of Tamil culture, language, and literature. The Justice

Party, another non–Brahmin organization, emerged in the 1920s stressing the Dravidian cultural nationalism and demanding separation of south India from the north. However, the party's appeal declined with the growing strength of the Congress-led Independence movement in the 1930s. The Dravida Munnetra Kazhagam (DMK) was another party formed by an amalgamation of several Dravidian groups in 1949 after India's Independence and was committed to the cause of non–Brahmins and Tamil identity and interests.

Thus, the context of India's Independence movement, the presence of social cleavages such as religion and ethnicity as well as the influence of communist ideology provided the backdrop for the emergence of diverse political organizations and parties despite the limited opportunities to participate in electoral politics in British India. After Independence, India's parliamentary democracy and the introduction of universal suffrage provided greater freedom for parties representing different ideologies and social groups to emerge and expand amidst an evolving political and party system.

Parties in Independent India

After Independence, J.P. Narayan, a former member of the Congress, and M.N. Roy, one of the founders of the CPI, called for a party-less Indian polity with the participation of the entire community, in order to have a true democracy uncorrupted by party politics. This idea, however, did not find much support, and parties in independent India continued to emerge and grow, and became an indispensable element of Indian democracy. The Congress was the most important political party in India at the time of Independence, with a robust party organization, and control over almost all the provincial assemblies and the Constituent Assembly that was entrusted with the drafting of India's Constitution. The Muslim League, the main opponent of the Congress in the pre-Independence period, became irrelevant in India after the creation of Pakistan in 1947. Other parties (for example the CPI, SAD) either did not have much experience of electoral politics or lacked a strong national party organization to provide a credible challenge to the Congress. The support for Bharatiya Jana Sangh (BJS), a new Hindu nationalist party formed in 1951, was limited to upper-caste middle-class voters, mainly in the Hindi-speaking northern states of the country.

Many new parties were formed during the 1950s and 1960s by dissident Congress factions. These included the Socialist Party, Kisan Mazdoor Praja Party (KMPP), Krishikar Lok Party (KLP), Bangla Congress, Kerala Congress, Swatantra Party, and Bharatiya Kranti Dal

11

(BKD). However, the opposition remained fragmented and relatively weak, and no party was in a position to challenge the Congress's dominance in the first two decades after India's Independence. In particular, there was uncertainty about which party was most capable to challenge the Congress, and the political environment remained fluid due to party splits and mergers. For example, after the first national election held in 1952, the KMPP and Socialist Party merged to form the Praja Socialist Party (PSP), which split again prior to the 1957 national election. Some parties which were opposed to the Congress were, however, able to gain strength in specific parts of the country, for example, the SAD in Punjab, DMK in Tamil Nadu, and Jammu and Kashmir National Conference (JKNC) in Jammu and Kashmir.

The 1960s saw the DMK making a transition from mainly being a party of an ethnic group—the non-Brahmins in Tamil Nadu—to a party of regional (Tamil) nationalism. It dropped its anti-Brahmin stance and projected itself as a party for all Tamil speakers. After the death of DMK's founder C.N. Annadurai (in 1969), the party split into two—the DMK and the All India Anna Dravida Munnetra Kazhagam (AIADMK) in 1972, both of which represented Tamil nationalism and became the main rival political parties in Tamil Nadu, displacing the Congress. JKNC, a regional political party in the state of Jammu and Kashmir, was founded in 1939 in pre-independent India by Sheikh Muhammad Abdullah. The party maintained that the state was an integral part of India, but also advocated for more autonomy for the state. In 1965, the JKNC merged with the Congress, but reverted to its separate identity in 1975. The party's influence has been confined to Jammu and Kashmir and it has had only a modest presence at the national level.

In the late 1960s and 1970s, the Congress's dominance started declining. Many parties were formed at the state level as part of the overall trend of consolidation of support in favour of the non-Congress parties. Although the Congress won the 1967 national election and formed the government at the centre, the opposition parties forged alliances and were able to form governments in several major Indian states. Many regional parties (parties with presence in one or few states) were formed based on support from a narrow social base. These included the Shiv Sena (SHS) in Maharashtra, formed in 1966, which positioned itself to promote and protect Maratha pride and culture, and the Jharkhand Mukti Morcha (JMM), formed in 1972 to represent the interests of the tribals in Bihar, and campaigned for the creation of a separate state of Jharkhand. Dissident members of the CPI formed the Communist Party of India (Marxist) or CPM in

1964, which opposed the state, the bourgeoisie, and the Congress party. Although CPM stressed extra-parliamentary methods during its early days, from the late 1960s it became more moderate, opposed radical strategies, and focused on electoral politics.

After being the dominant party for many years, the Congress witnessed a major split in 1969 when Prime Minister Indira Gandhi formed the Congress (R), the Congress (O) being the other Congress faction. The defections from the Congress continued to take place and the party was split into various other factions that were led by prominent Congress leaders. Charan Singh was one such leader who organized his own party, the BKD, in 1967 to serve the interests of the Jat caste of landowning farmers. In 1974, Bharatiya Lok Dal (BLD), led by Charan Singh, was formed through the merger of several parties opposed to the autocratic style of Indira Gandhi. These included the Swatantra Party; the Utkal Congress, a state party in Odisha; the BKD; and the Socialist Party. The anti-Congress agitation led by J.P. Narayan, and the subsequent imposition of national emergency by Indira Gandhi in 1975 culminated in the formation of the Janata Party by the merger of Congress (O), the BLD, the BJS, and the Socialist Party. Janata Party fought the 1977 national election, called after the revocation of national emergency, under the party label BLD and defeated the Congress to form the first non-Congress government at the centre in independent India. However, this government could not survive for the full term and fell in 1979, mainly due to personality clashes between the leaders of its constituent parties.

The disintegration of the Janata Party led to many new parties being formed in the 1980s and 1990s, which were launched by the leaders of its former constituents, prominent amongst them being the Lok Dal and Janata Dal (JD). The JD was formed in 1988 after the merger of Jan Morcha, which was a party formed by Congress dissidents, the rump Janata Party, and the two factions of the Lok Dal. However, the political situation remained fluid, where many of the offshoots of the former Janata Party continued to split or merge to form other parties, many of which continue to be in existence today, for example, the Samajwadi Party (SP) in Uttar Pradesh, Rashtriya Janata Dal (RJD) and Janata Dal (United) (JDU) in Bihar, Janata Dal (Secular) (JDS) in Karnataka, and Biju Janata Dal (BJD) in Odisha.

An electorally successful political party could not be formed around the Hindu religion in the pre-Independence era. After Independence, the BJS was formed in 1951, which stood for Hindu nationalism, but amalgamated into the Janata Party in 1977, playing an important role in the formation of the Janata government. After the fall of this government in 1979, the former members of the BJS formed a new party in 1980, the BJP, which grew to become one of the two main national parties in India in the 1990s and beyond.

The 1980s and 1990s also witnessed the formation of many parties that appealed to the voters primarily because of caste considerations. One such party was the Bahujan Samaj Party (BSP), which was formed in 1984 by Kanshi Ram to gain political power in order to provide adequate representation to members of Scheduled Castes (SCs; former untouchables or the Dalits), Scheduled Tribes (STs), and Other Backward Classes (OBC), as well as other religious and social minorities (together referred to as 'Bahujan Samaj' or the majority of the population). Caste was a significant social cleavage even before Independence, and B.R. Ambedkar, a legal scholar and a Dalit leader and activist, had demanded separate electorates for Dalit voters to fight caste divisions, which were awarded by the British in 1932. However, Gandhi found this idea to be divisive for the Hindu community within the context of his mass mobilization movement against the British and undertook a fast unto death in protest against this policy. This led to a settlement, where instead of having separate electorates, constituencies were reserved for lower caste candidates, but for whom the whole electorate in the constituency was eligible to vote. In 1936, Ambedkar founded the Independent Labour Party, which was succeeded in 1942 by the Scheduled Caste Federation, India's first political party formed with the objective of working for lower castes. Although this party was not particularly successful, its example inspired more electorally effective caste formations, including the BSP (Thachil 2014: 45).

The core support group of the BSP comprised primarily the Dalits (SCs) and it focused on the rights of the socially oppressed and marginalized sections of Indian society. Although Kanshi Ram was responsible for building the grass-roots support base of the party, it was Mayawati, his successor, who led it into being a major political force, especially in Uttar Pradesh. According to Chandra (2004: 184), an important reason for the emergence of the BSP was that SC activists and voters deserted the major parties in Uttar Pradesh and Punjab, where they were excluded from leadership positions, as soon as they were presented with a credible alternative of a caste-based party. In the 2000s, the BSP softened its agenda against the upper castes, with an aim to broaden its electoral support, especially in Uttar Pradesh. Although the BSP has been far more successful in Uttar Pradesh than in any other state, it fields a large number of candidates across the country in elections, and has tried to project itself as a national party. However, its support base is not geographically concentrated, which has limited its chances of national success due to the disproportionality (between vote and seat share) inherent in the SMPS. In addition to the BSP, many offshoots of the JD such as the RJD and JDU in Bihar, and SP in Uttar Pradesh, also actively mobilized voters primarily on caste lines, mainly drawing their support from the officially designated 'OBC', to emerge as politically significant regional parties in the 1990s.

Regional identity was another social cleavage, around which many political parties were formed after Independence. In Assam, Asom Gana Parishad (AGP) was launched as a regional political party in 1985, following a movement which demanded the deportation of illegal Bangladeshi nationals from the state. In Andhra Pradesh, a viable anti-Congress party did not emerge until the 1980s when the Telugu Desam Party (TDP), a regional party, was established in 1982 by a charismatic Telugu cinema actor N.T. Rama Rao. The decline of the Congress in the state, and the issue of respect for Telugu language and culture played an important part in the formation and success of TDP. Another party based on regional identity was Telangana Rashtra Samithi (TRS), which was formed in 2001 to represent the interests of people of the Telangana region of Andhra Pradesh and successfully led a movement for the creation of a new state of Telangana.

Two prominent new parties, the All India Trinamool Congress (AITC) and the Nationalist Congress Party (NCP), were formed in the 1990s by former members of the Congress. Founded in 1998, the AITC formed the government in West Bengal following the 2011 state assembly election, ending the 34-year rule of the CPM. It was founded by Mamata Banerjee, who had been a member of the Congress for over two decades. According to Palshikar (2003: 326), AITC emerged from an ambiguous scenario in West Bengal, where one faction of the Congress tried to associate with the all-India perception of politics leading to an anti-BJP strategy (effectively adopting a soft approach towards the Left front), while the other rooted its politics in the trajectory of state-level politics, which led to a tacit understanding with the BJP. The NCP was established in 1999 by three former members of the Congress led by Sharad Pawar, after they were expelled for demanding that only a person born in India should be allowed to become the country's president, vice president, or prime minister. The issue related to Sonia Gandhi, the Italian-born widow of the former Prime Minister Rajiv Gandhi, becoming the leader of the Congress. After its formation, the NCP, however, did not highlight this issue, and has allied with the Congress both in Maharashtra and at the centre. The NCP has had its greatest electoral success in Maharashtra, while its performance has been relatively less impressive in other states and at the national level.

Mufti Mohammed Sayeed, a former member of the Congress and later the JD, formed the Jammu and Kashmir Peoples Democratic Party (PDP) in 1999. After his death in 2016, his daughter Mehbooba Mufti took over as party leader. The PDP believes in self-rule as opposed to autonomy for the people of Jammu and Kashmir, and has been in power since 2015 in the state as part of a coalition government with the BJP.

The newest and, in many ways, a unique party formed in India after Independence, is the Aam Aadmi Party (AAP) or the common man's party. It was formed in 2012, having emerged out of an anti-corruption civil society movement—'India Against Corruption' (IAC) led by social activist Anna Hazare and his associates. However, the movement suffered a split, and in 2012, a section led by Arvind Kejriwal, a close aide of Hazare, decided to form a political party—AAP—while Hazare and his other supporters decided to remain outside electoral politics. It achieved a major victory in the 2015 Delhi state assembly election defeating both the Congress and the BJP, and is currently in power with Kejriwal as the chief minister.

Thus, many new parties have been formed after India's Independence on the basis of the social cleavages of caste, region, and religion as well as from splits and mergers of existing parties, often led by already successful leaders with aspirations to launch their own parties. According to Ziegfeld (2016: 168), the majority of these parties have broadly followed one of the following three trajectories. First, many parties have remained regional parties because of their founders' limited geographic influence, for example the BJD. The second category consists of parties with national aspirations, but which have not managed to expand beyond a regional base, for example, SP and NCP, while the third trajectory consists of short-lived national parties that either dissolved or disintegrated into regional parties, for example, Swatantra Party and JD. Figure 1.1 provides a timeline of the formation of major parties in India.

Typology of Parties and Party Systems

Political parties can be categorized on the basis of various dimensions, for example, ideology, support base, organization, type of leadership, and membership, and party systems can vary depending on the types of parties constituting it. One feature of the party system that has been used in the literature to categorize parties is the ideological distance between the parliamentary parties. Sartori (1976: 120) discusses the level of polarization that correlates with the type of party

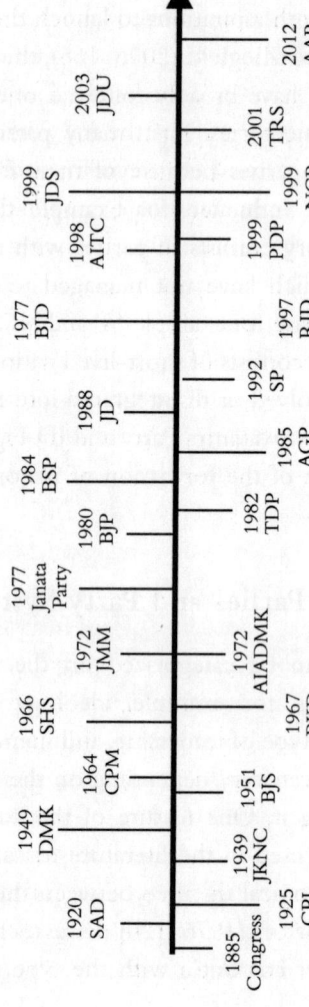

FIGURE 1.1 Timeline of Formation of Major Parties in India, 1885–2012

Source: Author's collation.

competition—centripetal or centrifugal. In a party system based on a centripetal tendency, parties tend to converge towards a centrist political position, while centrifugal drive involves a persistent loss of voters to one of the extreme ends of the ideological space. Another feature employed to categorize party systems is the number of parties competing in a polity, following which the numerical measures of the size of the party systems have become widely used in comparative politics literature.

Political parties in India vary in terms of size, ideology, and the way they appeal to the electorate, leading to different typologies based on various dimensions. For example, Indian parties have been categorized as secular, religion-based, catch-all, caste-based, ethnic, socialist, conservative, national, regional, and so on. Since many of these dimensions overlap in a significant manner, categorizing Indian parties in neat typologies is not a straightforward exercise.

Gunther and Diamond (2001: 10–11) provide five broad categories of political parties—elite, mass-based, ethnicity-based, electoralist, and movement parties. While elite parties consist of parties of local notables, and are weakly organized and mobilize support mainly through personal resources of the notables, mass-based parties are well-organized and have a mass membership, for example, from working classes, farmers, members of a specific religion, and so on. Ethnicity-based parties either cater to the interests of a narrowly defined ethnic group or mobilize support across wider multi-ethnic sections of the society. Electoralist parties can be personalistic, programmatic, or catch-all parties that are organizationally thin, and are election-oriented. Lastly, movement parties evolve from social movements and have distinct, often issue-based, political programmes.

Sridharan and DeSouza (2006: 18–20) apply this typology to categorize parties in the Indian context. Based on this categorization, the Congress can be defined as a multiethnic party that developed as an electoralist catch-all party from the late 1960s. The Congress also fits the description of a movement party, since it led India's Independence movement against the British colonial rule. BJP can be viewed as an ethnic party that has tried to move in the direction of becoming a catch-all party due to electoral compulsions. The communist parties, the CPI and CPM, are mass parties, but are more like social democratic, worker–peasant parliamentary parties in practice. Many parties that emerged from the 'Janata family', for example, the SP, RJD, BJD, JDU, and JDS, have the elements of catch-all, electoralist, and ethnicity-based parties. Some parties that have emerged from splits in the Congress, for example, the AITC, are more electoralist, often dominated by a charismatic leader. Parties such as the DMK,

AIADMK, SAD, and TDP are ethnicity-based parties with a regional ethnic character, but act as programmatic or catch-all electoralist parties within their states. The BSP can be considered as an ethnicity-based, programmatic electoralist party, which has increasingly become a personalistic party under Mayawati. The AAP, which was formed in 2012, can be viewed as a movement party with a personalistic, electoralist character.

Thachil and Teitelbaum (2015) provide a subcategorization of ethnic parties that rely on distributing excludable benefits to co-ethnics, rather than on providing public goods to all, into encompassing and narrow ethnic parties (NEP). While encompassing ethnic parties (EEP) target a broader ethnic core, the NEP emerge along identity categories shared by narrower sections of the electorate. Therefore, EEP tend to spend on broader public goods, whereas the NEP follow narrow patronage-based strategies within their restricted ethnic cores. Based on this typology, the AGP, AIADMK, DMK, SAD, and TDP are examples of the EEP, while the BSP, RJD, SP and SHS can be categorized as NEP.

Another typology categorizes parties based on characteristics such as ideology, movement, societal group interests, and party as an organization and party as government (Sridharan and DeSouza 2006: 21–3).

Thus, parties that emerged on purely ideological lines in India are the Communist parties on the Left, whose ideology lies in the Marxist–Leninist tradition, but can also be seen as parties of labour and peasant movements representing the working class and the poor farmers. On the Right, parties such as the BJP and SHS focus on the ideology of Hindu nationalism. The Communist parties and the BJP have a tightly organized, centralized, hierarchical organizations. Some regional parties such as the DMK and AIADMK in Tamil Nadu, AGP in Assam, and JMM in Jharkhand originated in social movements. Then, there are ethnicity-based parties in India that cater to specific societal groups based on caste, region, language, or religion. Examples of such parties are the SAD, DMK, and AIADMK.

Kailash (2014a) makes a distinction between regionalist parties, which are active in and promote the interests of particular states, and regionally located parties, which are also relevant in a limited geographical area, but do not necessarily have a 'regionalist' agenda and may aspire to become polity-wide parties. Ziegfeld (2016: 37) provides a categorization of regional parties in India as regionalist parties, remnants of the JD, splinters from the Congress, Left parties, independents, other major regional parties, and micro parties. The main regionalist parties include the SAD, JKNC, DMK, SHS, AIADMK, JMM, TDP, and AGP, which typically confine their political activity to either a single state or a small set of neighbouring states, but vary in the extent to which they actively demand greater regional autonomy. The remnants of the JD include the SP, JDS, RJD, and JDU, most of which draw support from specific caste groups. The offshoots of the Congress include the AITC, NCP, and YSR Congress Party (YSRCP), established in 2011. The main major Left parties are the CPI, All India Forward Bloc, and CPM, which have largely retained their basic ideology and tend not to be as closely defined with specific leaders or castes. Other regional parties include All India Majlis-e-Ittehadul Muslimeen (All India Council of the Union of Muslims), largely confined to the city of Hyderabad in Telangana, and Pattali Makkal Katchi (PMK), a caste-based party in Tamil Nadu which was established in 1989 (Ziegfeld 2016: 37–49).

According to Sridharan (2014: 49), the major parties in India are either national or regional and can be broadly categorized as secular parties, such as the Congress; Hindu nationalists such as the BJP and SHS; Communist parties such as the CPI and CPM; agrarian/lower-caste populist such as the SP, RJD, JD; ethnic/ethno-regional parties such as the DMK and AIADMK; and parties focused on specific castes or social groups, for example, the BSP and JMM.

While explaining which parties are most likely to provide private welfare to win over poor voters, Thachil (2014: 17) refers to two criteria common to most party typologies—the social profile of a party's core constituencies and the depth of its organizational resources. Thus, parties with less privileged cores, for example, Leftist populist and low-rank ethnic parties, can create redistribution strategies without alienating their core support base. However, not all of these parties have the resources to adopt such a strategy (the erstwhile Swatantra Party being a prominent example), and only those parties that combine an elite social base with thick organizational assets, for example, the BJP, are likely to use private welfare as an electoral strategy.

Although, ideologically, Indian political parties can be characterized based on the Left–Right dimension, due to the pluralism of Indian society, there is a compelling centripetal force driving the parties seeking power towards persistent centrism. In particular, due to a combination of India's social diversity, a multiparty system working within the institutional framework of SMPS and federalism, parties have incentives for propagating moderate views. This has led to a plural party system, not a sharply polarized one, especially at the national level (Sridharan and Varshney 2001). Even parties like the BJP and CPM, which were considered ideologically rigid parties, have over the years become more pragmatic in their electoral appeals and strategies.

The ideological moderation of the parties can be understood in the context of the 'median voter' theory, which prompts the parties to adapt policies and agenda towards the views of the median voter. This follows the Downsian or the proximity model of electoral competition, according to which each voter ranks candidates based on the proximity of their views, and is expected to lead to more centrist candidates and public policies due to the convergence to the centre ground (Hindmoor 2006). In general, there has been a narrowing of ideological positions adopted by parties in India. Further, the construction and shaping of an electorally viable social cleavage at the state or the national level seems challenging, giving parties an incentive to appear like a catch-all party (Palshikar et al. 2014: 22).

Many political parties in India are 'dynastic' where the leadership positions are usually held by members of a particular family. Chhibber (2013) argues that absence of a party organization, independent civil society associations that mobilize support for the party, and centralized financing of elections has led to the emergence and sustenance of dynastic parties in India. Chandra (2016a) notes that the causes of dynastic politics in India relate to the large returns associated with state office and the organizational weakness of political parties. The Congress is a prime example of a dynastic party where the top leadership roles have, in most part, remained within the Nehru–Gandhi family. Many regional parties, for example, the SAD, SHS, NCP, DMK, TDP, BJD, SP, RJD, NC, and PDP also exhibit characteristics of a dynastic party. The non–dynastic parties, in contrast, draw their leadership from the wider party membership; prominent non-dynastic parties in India include the BJP, CPI, CPM, and AAP.

Yadav and Palshikar (2006) stress the need to distinguish between changes in the party system and changes in the prospects of the parties constituting it. They present a typology of party systems in the Indian states based on the interaction of the format of party competition (evidenced by the number of competing parties) and the nature of political choices offered by the parties that could determine the possibility of social transformation through democratic means. These party system types are: unipolar hegemony, bipolar convergence, multipolar convergence, competitive divergence, one-party domination, closed one-party system, and system-less competition, which represent 'ideal types' specific to a time period and/or one or more Indian states. Yadav and Palshikar (2006) argue that despite a large number of Indian states having shifted to a two-party or multiparty competition, the 'convergence' or tendency of major parties to become like one another has led to the disappearance of issues with transformative potential from the political agenda.

Determinants of the Number of Parties in a Polity

Existing studies on the determinants of the number of parties in a polity has been dominated by two approaches. The institutional approach stresses the role of institutional rules such as the electoral system in determining the number of parties expected in a polity (Cox 1997; Duverger 1963 [1954]), while the sociological approach treats the size of the party system as a reflection of social cleavages (Lipset and Rokkan 1967). Another approach stresses the interaction between sociological and institutional factors to explain the size of the party system in a polity (Neto and Cox 1997). Further, contextual factors such as the effect of fiscal and political centralization by the national government (Chhibber and Kollman 2004), dependence of states on the central government (Diwakar 2010), the type of party leadership, and the overall political environment also shape the size of the party system.

The institutional approach has most notably been represented by 'Duverger's Law', according to which a simple-majority single-ballot system favours the two-party system (Duverger 1963 [1954]). This outcome is linked to 'strategic voting' by voters whereby they do not waste their votes, and instead prefer to vote for a candidate who has a chance of winning the election. Duverger's law is normally expected to work at the constituency level, where the elections are actually contested. Thus, even when social cleavages may give rise to a higher number of parties that contest elections, under a non-permissive electoral system such as the SMPS, voters are expected to support two parties, which receive all or most of the votes in a constituency. Chhibber and Kollman (2004) find evidence for a general prevalence of Duverger's Law in many countries, including India, at the constituency level. Sridharan (2002) concludes that Duverger's Law seems to hold true at the state level in India, but not at the national level.

Other institutional factors such as federalism, laws regulating parties such as the Anti-Defection Law, 1985, and the rules that are used to shape the internal structure of political parties also have important consequences for the Indian party system (Wyatt 2009). Diwakar (2007) finds that Duverger's Law does not hold true at the national level and, even at the constituency level, there is no unequivocal support for its predictions in India. She argues that a narrow focus on institutional rules is inadequate and a more comprehensive set of variables is needed to explain the size of the Indian party system.

According to the sociological school, the number of parties reflect the social diversity in a polity, and, therefore, a country with a higher number of social groups or cleavages is likely to have a larger number of parties to represent them (Lipset and Rokkan 1967). Despite India's Partition on the basis of religion, it still inherited a highly heterogeneous population with a multitude of castes, linguistic, ethnic, and religious groups. In this scenario, politicization of religion, caste, and region have given rise to the formation and growth of many parties, for example, the BJP (Hindu nationalism), BSP (caste), JMM (tribe), DMK and AIADMK (cultural identity), and SHS (nativism) on the basis of various social cleavages. Mehra (2003) argues that the party system acquires a special connotation in multicultural societies where parties represent multiple groups and interests, and need to engage in coalition building at national and state levels. This is especially true in the Indian case, where parties compete and engage at various levels, and give rise to diverse party systems across the Indian states.

Since both social cleavages and electoral rules tend to be stable, the change in the number of parties over time has been explained by the degree of fiscal and political centralization exercised by the central government (Chhibber and Kollman 2004). Accordingly, in periods of centralization of power in the hands of central government, the voters tend to vote for larger party labels, and this leads to party aggregation at the national level and decentralization phases see party disaggregation at the national level in the Indian case. Extending this theory, Diwakar (2010) has shown that Indian states that are highly dependent on the national government for resources respond more strongly to federal centralization and have fewer number of parties.

Many Indian parties tend to display a more top-down centralized approach towards decision-making, and lack internal democracy which makes party leadership a key contextual factor in shaping parties and the party system in India. The importance of political leadership has been well illustrated by the contribution of 'political entrepreneurs' to the emergence of new parties in the state of Tamil Nadu (Wyatt 2009). Further, since the 1990s, the expectation of a coalition government, especially at the centre, has incentivized the formation of smaller regional parties, and has been another important contextual factor in determining the size of the Indian party system (Ziegfeld 2016).

Finally, the party system in India has been and continues to be shaped by unexpected events, for example, the imposition of national emergency by

Prime Minister Indira Gandhi in 1975, her assassination in 1984 and later of her son Rajiv Gandhi in 1991, and the emergence of new politically salient issue dimensions, for example, corruption, which led to the establishment of a new party—the AAP in 2012.

Consequences of Party Systems

Parties and party systems have important political, social, and economic consequences, for example, on government formation and durability and the provision of public goods. The size and the competitiveness of the party systems are important determinants of voters getting meaningful electoral choices, and a country getting a stable government. As Yadav and Palshikar (2006: 74) argue, 'the party system defines the structure of political competition that shapes and constraints the political choices that a citizen can exercise'. In the Indian context, one has seen that fragmented legislatures and coalition governments find it more difficult to frame and pass laws, and implement policies. Chhibber and Nooruddin (2004) find that Indian states with two-party competition provide more public goods than ones with multiparty competition. This happens because in two-party systems parties draw support from many social groups, and therefore need to provide more public goods to win elections.

In multiparty systems, on the other hand, parties only need a plurality of votes to win an election, and therefore are more likely to use private goods rather than public goods to mobilize electoral support. Similarly, according to Saez and Sinha (2010), an increase in the number of parties, which represents the extent of party competition in a polity, has a positive effect on education expenditure by the Indian states.

India currently has a multiparty system, with a variety of parties representing a range of ideologies and many social cleavages such as caste, religion, ethnicity, and region. Although the Congress emerged as a dominant party and the natural choice for governance at the time of India's Independence due to a range of factors, new parties have continued to form, including by the splits and mergers of existing parties.

2

The Congress 'System' and Its Decline

The Congress's pre-eminent position as a national party at the time of India's Independence in 1947 contributed significantly towards a relatively undifferentiated party system across most states of India until 1967. As a consequence, the politics and party systems in the states were commonly viewed as an extension of national politics, rather than having their own distinct characteristics. However, this feature of the Indian party system began to change in the 1970s and 1980s, as many new parties emerged to challenge the Congress at the state level, and also began to influence national politics, although on a limited basis. Analysing the nature of the party system and the factors that shaped it in this phase is important to understand the evolution of the Indian party system thereafter.

Congress's Role before India's Independence

The Congress was the first mass-based political organization in India, which emerged from the nationalist
movement against British colonial rule. It was founded
in 1885 at the initiative of a retired British civil ser-
vant, A.O. Hume. Its first session was attended by 72
delegates from all over India, and its pan-Indian and
secular character made this gathering unprecedented.
These delegates were well-educated and largely represented the professions of law, journalism, and teaching.
The key objective of the Congress at the time of its
formation was to provide a platform for a dialogue
between educated Indians and the British. It also aimed
to demand better representation of Indians in the civil
service and to bring about administrative and judicial
reforms. Since Congress's demands seemed reasonable,
non-revolutionary, and placed within the context of
the framework of the continuation of British rule in
India, there was limited opposition against its formation from the British colonial government.

In the first two decades of its existence, the Congress
lacked a systematic organizational structure and a mass
appeal, and largely remained loyal to the British Crown.
In 1915, M.K. Gandhi (who was later also known as
Mahatma Gandhi), a young Indian lawyer and a civil
rights campaigner for Indians in South Africa, returned

to India, and under his leadership the Congress gradually moved from being an urban, middle-class, loyalist organization to a mass political movement beginning in the 1920s, representing a broader church of opinions and interests. Under Gandhi, the party became the leading political organization in India's Independence movement against the British rule, and emerged as a unifying national force in a large and diverse country. Gandhi's initial strategy included developing a new organizational structure for the Congress, with the main objective of attaining self-government through lawful means within the British Commonwealth. During the period between the 1920s and India's Independence in 1947, the Congress's strategy and activities went through a series of distinct cycles (Metcalf and Metcalf 2006: 184). These usually began with an act of provocation by the British, to which the Congress responded through a programme of civil disobedience led by Gandhi. The British then reacted to this defiance through a strategy of providing concessions, as well as further suppression, for example, through arresting members of the Congress.

Besides the Congress, there were also other political parties in India, which emerged in the pre-Independence era. The Congress's principal political opponent was the Muslim League, which was founded in 1906, but its support was highly dispersed, varying with the presence of the Muslim population in India. Initially, it lobbied the British to protect the rights of the Muslims, but from the 1930s it focused its efforts towards the creation of an independent country, for Muslims, that is, Pakistan. The SAD represented the Sikhs and its influence was limited to the Punjab province where the Sikh community was concentrated. The Unionist Party in Punjab represented a coalition of Sikh, Hindu, and Muslim landed interests. The CPI emerged in the 1920s, but largely remained outside electoral politics, concentrating instead on building a cadre and creating a movement parallel to the Congress's civil disobedience against the British rule. The Justice Party was another party, which was electorally active in the 1920s and 1930s, and mainly promoted the interests of non-Brahmins in the Madras province.

The transformation of the Congress from a mass movement into a mainstream political party got a fillip in 1937, when it participated in the elections to the provincial legislatures following the 1935 Government of India Act. This act gave a limited degree of self-government to the 11 provinces of British India, although the provincial legislatures continued to share power with the British at the all-India level. The Congress achieved major success in these elections, winning 711 of 1,585 seats in the provincial legislatures, and formed governments in 7 out of 11 British Indian provinces. When in office, these provincial governments worked with the British provincial governors, and its leaders gained experience in the practice of government, as opposed to politics of agitation. In 1939, the British declared that India was joining the war against Germany without consulting the provincial legislatures. The Congress ministries resigned against this unilateral declaration and Britain's unwillingness to agree to a speedy independence in return for India's cooperation during the war.

After the 1946 provincial elections, the Congress formed the government in 8 of the 11 provinces, while the Muslim League was successful in forming governments in 2 provinces. In the Punjab province, a coalition government of the Congress, Unionists, and SAD was formed. One of the principal objectives of these elections was to provide the basis for the election of a Constituent Assembly for an independent Indian Union, by the new provincial assemblies. The Muslim League decided to boycott the early sessions of the Constituent Assembly, effectively making it a Congress-dominated forum. J.L. Nehru and V. Patel of the Congress were two prominent members of the Constituent Assembly, who later became the first prime minister and home minister of independent India, respectively. Outside the Congress, B.R. Ambedkar was another influential member of the Constituent Assembly, who was also the chairman of the drafting committee of the Indian Constitution.

India's Partition in 1947 into two sovereign countries—India and Pakistan—increased the influence of the Congress party in the provincial assemblies of Bengal and Punjab, where it was not the leading party. In Bengal, the largest party after the 1946 election was the Muslim League, and in Punjab the main non-Congress parties were the Unionist Party, SAD, and Muslim League. While the Muslim League became the leading party in Pakistan and therefore irrelevant in India, the Unionist Party effectively ceased to exist as Muslim Unionists integrated into the Muslim League. Consequently, the Congress emerged as a dominant party in Bengal, and with an upper hand relative to the SAD in Punjab. Thus, by the time British left India, the Congress had almost full control over all the provincial assemblies, which gave it a dominant position within the Indian state, and a virtual monopoly over state patronage. As Desai (2009: 297) states, the Congress by this time, 'had become an election-winning and power-using machine', and did not follow Gandhi's advice to disband itself as a political party and instead become a social service agency after Independence.

According to Tudor (2013: 119–23), the Congress's electoral and governing success in the pre-Independence decades was due to an intra-party organization which provided an effective mechanism for channelling grass-roots support into a relatively streamlined but democratic leadership. The party was also able to substantially improve its financial position after 1920 and succeeded in expanding its membership, especially in the rural regions of India. Thus, India emerged from Independence with a party that was effectively able to contain factionalism and accommodate ethnic differences (Tudor 2003: 21).

Congress 'System' or Dominance, 1952–67

After Independence, the Congress became a large pan-Indian political organization, which operated at all levels of the country's political landscape. The transformation of the Congress from a mass nationalist movement, with an aim of winning power from the British, into a political party also altered the role performed by its members. Accordingly, the party had to adapt its organization for winning electoral support, and develop a mechanism for dealing with inter- and intra-party conflicts. To do so, Congress leaders sought to combine traditional party roles and values of conciliation and consensus in order to maintain its pivotal role in the Indian party and political system. India's Independence movement had enabled the mobilization of a large section of the country's population, and, in a sense, prevented the politicization of local divisions and social cleavages except religion, which too became less relevant, at least in the initial years after the formation of Pakistan. Even after Independence, potential sources of political mobilization such as region, religion, caste, and ideological divisions such as Left versus Right or modern versus traditional remained relatively dormant during the phase of the Congress's dominance.

The prominent role of the Congress in the Independence movement, and the limited interest and experience of opposition parties in electoral politics provided a major advantage to the party, which contributed to its dominance in the initial decades after Independence. The party also gained because of its country-wide organizational structure. New parties that emerged out of Congress factions lacked the organization, resources, and geographical reach of the Congress. These included the Socialist Party, KMPP, and KLP, which later split or merged with other parties. Parties such as the BJS, which was founded in 1951 as the political wing of the Hindu organization—the RSS—and the CPI had limited experience or interest in electoral politics. Thus, due to the irrelevance of many of their opponents after Independence, and the relative inexperience, limited reach, and resources of the new parties that emerged, India's early post-Independence elections saw a fragmented opposition competing against the Congress. As a result, the Indian party system between 1952 and 1967, both at the national level and the state level, was largely defined by and centred on the Congress.

In the first four national elections held in 1952, 1957, 1962, and 1967, the Congress won an average of 69 per cent of seats and 45 per cent of votes. It also won the majority of seats in most of the state assembly elections, which were held concurrently with the national elections to the Lok Sabha. Despite facing multiparty competition, the Congress successfully held a place in the middle of the political centre ground, as a catch-all party, and emerged as the winner in the national and most state assembly elections held during this period. As a result, the party enjoyed unshared governmental power at the centre and in most states, even though it never won a majority of votes in the national elections.

An insightful explanation of the Indian party system during this period was offered by Kothari (1964), who defined it as a 'system' of 'one-party dominance', and not a one-party system, and one which was nevertheless competitive. According to this view, the Congress system comprised a 'party of consensus', which was the Congress, including its internal factions, and the 'parties of pressure', the opposition parties that functioned on the margin and created the 'margin of pressure'. Both the ideas of an inbuilt corrective mechanism through factions within the Congress, and a latent threat from outside the margin of pressure were necessary parts of this Congress-dominated party system. While the plurality of views within the Congress made it more representative and provided the party with the flexibility and capacity to manage internal competition, the fragmented opposition acted as a constant threat to its dominance, but without the ability to be a viable alternative. Consequently, most political conflicts and debates in the Indian political scene took place within the Congress itself, rather than between the Congress and the opposition parties. In such an environment, the Congress was able to internalize political competition, and represented a unique kind of historical consensus amongst diverse political views.

Kothari (1964) also delineated how the Congress system was strengthened after India's Independence. The party provided for an important role for the government in nation building, made central authority a key feature of national politics, and also concentrated economic power and state patronage in its hands. The Congress system could sustain itself because of a 'conciliatory machinery', which mediated factional disputes and influenced political decisions, thus confirming its position of patronage and power. Such a position of the Congress was also strengthened by its strategy of neutralizing the effects of narrow social cleavages and disaffection.

According to Morris-Jones (1966), the Congress system during this phase was characterized by 'openness' of three distinct kinds—the Congress being open to a fairly free movement in and out of the organization; the party being open to other parties to enter the competition for power; and the party having openness in positively communicating and interacting with other parties. According to this view, the Congress could be conceived as a circle whose midpoint was at the intersection of all the principal axes of polarization. The opposition parties were positioned outside the Congress circle, diametrically opposed to each other along various axes, but were closer to Congress factions adjacent to them on their axes than to other opposition parties. Since the Congress system was a competitive and an open one, the opposition parties were able to engage with, and influence the sections of the Congress which were ideologically close to these parties. However, despite achieving a combined vote share of more than 50 per cent in the national elections, the opposition parties were neither able to alternate with the Congress in the exercise of power, nor share power as part of a coalition due to a fragmented and geographically dispersed support base.

It is important to note that despite the Congress being the dominant party, the Congress government functioned as a democratic establishment, and not as an authoritarian regime. The sustenance of democracy was facilitated because of the democratic ideals of founding fathers of the party. Nehru, an eminent political personality and India's first prime minister was, in particular, credited for promoting and preserving democratic culture and institutions during this period.

The dominance of the Congress can also be understood as a phase of transition, where a new nation was establishing itself as a democracy within a highly heterogeneous society, with a single party acting like an agent between the state and its people. The Congress system sought to relate the mechanics of this model—for example, intra-party competition, inter-party competition, and the intimate relation between the two—with its historical dynamics, including its nation-building ethos, the changing role of the government, control of economic power, and mobilization of new social groups into the political mainstream through both the openness of the participatory structure and the use of public policies (Kothari 1970). At the national level, opposition parties functioned through a series of links with factional alliances within the Congress, and at the state level, these parties related to various factions within the Congress governments as well as the Congress state organizations.

According to Riker (1982), in most elections it contested, the Congress was a 'Condorcet winner', the candidate or the party which, when compared with every other candidate, is preferred by most voters. The Congress, as the largest single party, included the ideological median of voters and had been the second choice of many voters on both its Right and Left. Therefore, it emerged as a Condorcet winner since it probably would have been able to defeat Rightists in a pairwise contest because Leftists would vote for the Congress rather than Rightists, and, similarly, it would have been able to defeat Leftists in a pairwise contest because Rightists would vote for the Congress rather than Leftists. Similarly, Lijphart (1996) argued that the Congress could be thought of as being a grand coalition, whose success was brought about and sustained by power-sharing in a heterogeneous society, Condorcet winning, and the internal democracy practised in the Congress.

A counter view has been presented by Chhibber and Petrocik (1989) who argue that the Congress was not a Condorcet winner, but reflected particular social cleavages such as caste, class, and religion. Since all these cleavages could not be translated across states, the opposition parties did not have a consistent support base, and, therefore, their growth was limited by regional boundaries. Hewitt (2008) also notes that the socio-economic basis of the Congress's electoral support differed from state to state, and that such differentiation allowed the party to represent a national mandate based upon quite different, and, in some cases, even mutually opposed social cleavages.

Thus, the mobilization strategy of the Congress to cultivate different social sections in different parts of the country was based on the party using a national- ist appeal and stressing the need to keep the country united. This macro-level or 'master' nationalist cleav- age (Yadav and Palshikar 2006) made the mobilization based on other social cleavages and divisions by non- Congress parties a difficult proposition. Although some parties attempted to construct their support based on potential divisions in the society, for example, the BJS pursuing a Hindu constituency, the Swatantra Party attempting to win support in the ex-princely states, and the SAD's association with the Sikhs in Punjab, these efforts were in contrast with the Congress' pan- India mobilization strategy, and therefore remained confined to specific regions or sections of the society.

The domination of the Congress was dependent on its effectiveness in distributing the resources which it acquired from its control of state power. Its monopoly over state patronage and resources also enabled the party to manage grievances, which had the potential of being politicized by the opposition. Another factor behind the party's success was its state-based leaders and chief ministers, who were relatively autonomous and functioned without major interference from the central government. The Congress also benefitted from the institutional mechanism of concurrent holding of national and state elections, where national issues could overshadow local issues, thus giving the party an advantage over regional parties.

Finally, Congress's dominance during this phase was also due to the effects of the SMPS, which usually favours larger parties at the cost of electorally unviable smaller parties. This advantage manifests in a party winning a larger share of seats than its share of votes, commonly referred to as 'seat bonus'. While the Congress secured a majority of seats in the parliament, it did so without winning the majority of votes, benefitting from an average seat bonus of 24 per cent during the period 1952–67.

Table 2.1 illustrates that the Congress remained the dominant party both in respect of seats and votes won in the national elections held during the period 1952–67, although its share of seats declined sharply in 1967. This pattern is also evident by observing the Effective Number of Parties (ENP), which is a commonly used measure of the size of the party system in a polity. The ENP is computed by weighing the number of parties by their seats or votes share, following Laakso and Taagepera's (1979) formula

$$ENP = 1/[\Sigma pi^2]$$

where p represents vote or seat share of the ith party.

While ENP by seats indicates the relative strength of parties in the legislature, ENP by votes reflects the degree of the overall competitiveness of a party system. For both measures, higher values reflect a more competitive and fragmented nature of the party system. For example, an ENP of 3 indicates that the party system is as fragmented as if there were 3 equal-sized competing parties.

As shown in Table 2.1, ENP by seats remained below 2 during 1952–62 reflecting the Congress's dominance amidst a fragmented opposition, but it increased to 3.1 in the 1967 election. Further, despite the Congress winning a majority of seats in these elections, the ENP by votes never fell below 4 during this phase, reflecting a multiparty competitive system, based on the vote share received by parties.

Thus, the explanation of India's party system during the phase of the Congress's dominance is a stylized analysis, which stresses the importance of unique historical context and circumstances, and does not clearly fit the traditional models of either one

TABLE 2.1 Summary Results of National Elections (Lok Sabha), 1952–67

Party	Seat share (%)				Vote share (%)			
	1952	1957	1962	1967	1952	1957	1962	1967
Congress	74	75	73	54	45	48	45	41
Swatantra Party[2]	NA[1]	NA	4	8	NA	NA	8	9
Communist parties[3]	3	5	6	8	3	9	10	9
Socialist parties[4]	4	4	3	7	16	10	10	8
BJS	1	1	3	7	3	6	6	9
Other parties	10	6	7	9	17	8	10	10
Independents	8	9	4	7	16	19	11	14
ENP (by seat or votes)	1.7	1.7	1.9	3.1	4.5	4.0	4.4	5.2

Source: ECI election statistics and author's calculations.

Notes: 1. 'NA' means the party either did not exist or did not contest elections; 2. Swatantra Party was founded in 1959 to provide a Right-wing opposition to the Congress. In 1974, it merged into the Janata Party, an amalgamation of many anti-Congress parties; 3. The main Communist parties were the CPI, and after 1964, CPI and CPM; 4. These included the Socialist Party, KMPP, PSP, and Samyukta Socialist Party (SSP).

party or multiparty competition. Overall, contextual determinants such as the legitimacy of the Congress party, arising from its role in India's Independence, the strength of its organization and leadership under Nehru, monopoly over state patronage, and institutional factors such as SMPS and concurrent holding of national and state assembly elections were instrumental in shaping the nature of the Indian party system during this period. The sociological factors, on the other hand, remained relatively dormant due to Congress's centrist ideological position, the presence of an overarching nationalist cleavage, and Nehru's secular credentials.

Decline in the Congress's Dominance, 1967–89

After Nehru's death in 1964, the Congress system underwent many changes. It had to move away from its dependence on his charismatic leadership, and function amidst a worsening economic situation. L.B. Shastri, who had taken over as prime minister after Nehru, died suddenly in 1966, after which Indira Gandhi, Nehru's daughter, became the prime minister. After the 1967 national election, the Congress started losing support at the centre and in many states, and the party system began to become more diffused and differentiated across the Indian states. While previously political conflict had largely occurred and been contained within the Congress, it began to manifest itself in the form of inter-party electoral competition. Further, there began a period of regular defections, whereby leaders moved both in and out of the Congress. Overall, the Indian party system was evolving into another phase, in which the Congress had to function under more complex set of circumstances, where the opposition became less fragmented, new states were formed, and the economic environment underwent many changes.

The party suffered its first major split in 1969, and, as a result, it faced a more united opposition in the 1971 national election. Despite this split and a sharp decline in its seat and vote share in the 1967 election, Congress (R), the faction led by Indira Gandhi, won 44 per cent of the votes and 68 per cent of seats in the 1971 election. Indira Gandhi successfully exploited the macro-level issue of poverty, appealing to a particular class to neutralize other competing social divisions to achieve this electoral victory. The party's strategy under her also included building state-specific coalitions of different social groupings in different states.

After winning the 1971 national election, Indira Gandhi adopted a personalized style of leadership, which was built around projecting her status as the supreme party leader, centralizing power in herself, and filling positions in party organization through appointment rather than by election. This 'high-command' culture led to a relatively opaque style of decision-making within the party, and as a result, the Congress's traditional strength and powers as an effective organization eroded considerably. Indira Gandhi also became less tolerant of the opposition parties and opposition-controlled state governments. Thus, dissent within the party was seen as being anti-Congress, and attempts by opposition parties to mobilize public opinion against the Congress were perceived as a law-and-order problem, rather than a part of the democratic process. Eventually, this confrontationist style of functioning proved less capable of managing conflicts both within the party, and more generally, in a large, federal, and heterogeneous polity.

By 1974, this fluid situation led to the strengthening of an opposition-led movement against the Congress government, and, in particular, Indira Gandhi. This ultimately resulted in the imposition of national emergency by her in June 1975, which lasted until March 1977. During the Emergency, there was further central-ization of power in the hands of Indira Gandhi and her son Sanjay Gandhi, suspension of civil liberties, curtail-ment of the freedom of the press, and imprisonment of opposition leaders and activists. In the 1977 national election, which took place after this phase of emergen-cy rule, the Congress, for the first time, faced a united opposition in the form of the Janata Party (officially Bharatiya Lok Dal) and was comprehensively defeated. The Congress secured only 35 per cent of votes and 28 per cent of seats in the Lok Sabha. The Janata Party won a clear majority with 54 per cent of seats based on 41 per cent of votes. Although the Congress's electoral position had weakened after the 1967 national election, it was the 1977 election that marked the beginning of the end of the era of its dominance, when it lost power at the national level for the first time.

The Congress, which had also dominated the state-level elections until 1967, lost elections in several major states in 1977 and 1978. Overall, the years after 1977 saw regular alternation of power between parties at the state level, splits within the parties and, in general, a move towards a more fragmented party system both at the national and state level. In 1972, the Congress suspended elections to its party organization, which led to further centralization of power within the party. Its defeat in the 1977 national election also saw some of its prominent leaders in many states leaving the party to form new parties or join opposition parties, and the Congress became even more personalized under Indira Gandhi's leadership.

The Janata Party, which ran the national government during 1977–9 comprised a group of heterogeneous parties, which had joined together to present a united opposition to the Congress in the 1977 national election. It included the BJS, a few factions of the Congress which had broken away from it, and parties representing the farmers of India's Hindi-speaking regions. Due to its diverse composition and personality clashes between its top leaders, the Janata government did not last long and fell in 1979, leading to splintering of many of its former constituents into other parties. The BJP and Janata Party (secular), later known as Lok Dal, were prominent among these, thus leaving a substantially reduced Janata Party. Following the disintegration of the Janata Party, the Congress presented itself as the only viable national party to the electorate, and was able to win almost two-thirds of the seats in the 1980 national election, on the basis of a vote share of 43 per cent, with Indira Gandhi returning as the prime minister. Although the Congress returned to power with an overwhelming majority, this result rested more on the rejection of the unstable alternative pitted against it, rather than marking a return to a Congress-dominated party system.

The 1984 national election was held after the assassination of Indira Gandhi by two Sikh security guards in retaliation to 'Operation Blue Star' ordered by her in June 1984, which involved a military operation to remove armed militants from the Golden Temple, a holy place of the Sikhs in Amritsar, Punjab. The

Congress contested this election under the leadership of Rajiv Gandhi, Indira Gandhi's son, and riding on a sympathy wave, won 49 per cent of the votes and almost 80 per cent of the Lok Sabha seats. This win was also attributed to the continuing failure of opposition parties to provide a credible alternative, and to the fresh appeal of a youthful Rajiv Gandhi.

Although the 1977 election marked an important milestone in the decline of the dominance of the Congress in Indian politics, it continued as the most important, although not the dominant, national party, winning the next two national elections in 1980 and 1984, even as the party system became more competitive. Despite these victories in the national elections, party system in many states had already developed or were developing distinct patterns, independent of political trends seen at the national level. This was due to the rise of regional parties, some of which were also led by defectors from the Congress. These included the states of Tamil Nadu, West Bengal, Kerala, Andhra Pradesh, Haryana, and Karnataka. The states of Punjab and Assam witnessed political unrest and militancy, which was another challenge to the Congress-centred party system. The growth of state-specific parties and party systems was also facilitated by the delinking of national and state assembly elections since the 1971 national election. The 1989 national election marked

an unequivocal end to the era of the Congress's dominance, when it suffered a defeat against an electoral
alliance—the National Front (NF) comprising many
parties, which resulted in low fragmentation of the
anti-Congress votes. The main constituents of NF
were JD at the national level, TDP of Andhra Pradesh,
DMK of Tamil Nadu, and AGP of Assam.

Table 2.2 summarizes the results of the national
elections held between 1971 and 1989, period which
largely corresponds with the phase of 'Congress-
opposition system' (Yadav 1996), when the Congress's
seat share declined from 68 per cent to 37 per cent, and
its domination came under attack from a more united
opposition.

At the state level too, many parties had emerged by
1989 to provide credible alternatives to the Congress,
which no longer remained a natural choice for the
electorate. As a result, the party system at the state level
saw a gradual consolidation of the non-Congress opposition. This led to the displacement of the Congress as
one of the two leading parties in many states. However,
the pattern of consolidation of the opposition against
the Congress varied between states, as well as between
national and state assembly elections, but in general,
the party's electoral losses were heavier in the state
assembly elections (Sridharan 2002). In some states, for
example, Madhya Pradesh and Rajasthan, there was a

TABLE 2.2 Summary Results of National Elections (Lok Sabha), 1971–89

Party	Seat share (%)					Vote share (%)				
	1971	1977	1980	1984	1989	1971	1977	1980	1984	1989
Congress	68	28	67	79	37	44	35	43	49	40
Communist parties[2]	9	5	9	5	9	10	7	8	9	9
Bharatiya Janata Party	NA[1]	NA	NA	–	16	NA	NA	NA	8	11
Janata Party/BLD[3]	NA	54	NA	NA	NA	NA	41	NA	NA	NA
Janata Dal[4]	NA	NA	NA	NA	27	NA	NA	NA	NA	18
Janata Party (S)[5]	NA	NA	8	NA	NA	NA	NA	9	NA	NA
Janata Party[6]	NA	NA	NA	2	NA	NA	NA	19	7	NA
Other parties	20	11	8	13	9	38	11	15	19	17
Independents	3	2	2	1	2	8	6	6	8	5
ENP (by seats or votes)	2.1	2.6	2.3	1.7	4.1	5.2	3.4	4.2	3.8	4.8

Source: ECI election statistics and author's calculations.

Notes: 1. NA means the party either did not exist or did not contest election, and '–' means no seats won; 2. These include CPI and CPM; 3. This was an amalgamation of many anti-Congress parties, which contested under the label BLD; 4. JD was formed in 1988 by merger of various parties that were part of Janata Party/BLD, few other parties; 5. Janata Party (S) was a faction of Janata Party/BLD; 6. This was the rump Janata Party after the Janata Party/BLD disintegrated into factions. BJP won 2 seats in 1984.

movement towards a consolidation of non-Congress vote behind the BJP. In other states, for example, West Bengal and Kerala, the Congress on its own or in alliance with a state party competed against a coalition of Left parties—CPM and CPI. In many states, for example, Andhra Pradesh, Punjab, Assam, and Jammu and Kashmir, a bipolar party system comprising the Congress and a regional party emerged.

The Congress was also displaced from being one of the two leading parties in the state of Tamil Nadu, where a transition into competition between the two state parties—DMK and AIADMK—took place. In the relatively smaller states of Nagaland, Manipur, Mizoram, Meghalaya, and Sikkim in the Northeast, a two-party system involving competition between the Congress and regional parties emerged. The Congress continued to be a major party until 1989 in many large states where opposition could not consolidate against it, for example, Uttar Pradesh, Maharashtra, Gujarat, Bihar, Karnataka, Haryana, and Odisha (Sridharan 2002).

Figure 2.1 highlights the Congress's performance in the national elections of 1967, 1977, and 1989, which marked important milestones in the period of the Congress-dominated party system. While 1967 election results showed that Congress domination was weakening, the 1977 election was the first time the party lost a national election. However, it was the 1989

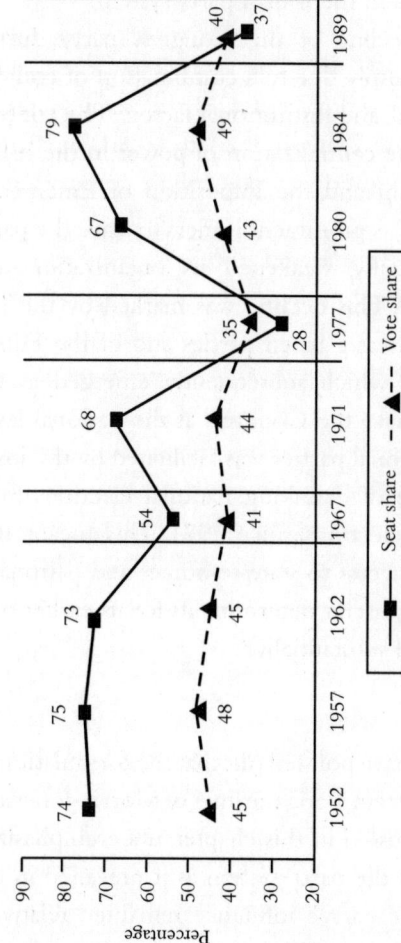

FIGURE 2.1 Vote Share and Seat Share Won by the Congress in the Lok Sabha, 1952–89

Source: Author's calculations based on ECI election statistics.

election that marked the end of the central role played by the Congress in the Indian party system.

Thus, the decline of the Congress party during 1967–89 was mainly due to a combination of contextual, sociological, and institutional factors. The contextual factor of the centralization of power in the hands of Indira Gandhi and the imposition of Emergency caused many of its prominent leaders to leave the party, which substantially weakened its organization and electoral appeal. This decline was marked by the rise of regional and caste-based parties and of the Hindu nationalist BJP, which subsequently emerged as the main challenger to the Congress at the national level. The rise of regional parties was facilitated by the institutional change of delinking national elections from state assembly elections since 1971. This meant that the Congress's access to state resources and patronage, which were important determinants for its earlier success, diminished substantially.

Some scholars have pointed out that the formulation of the Congress system along the lines of Morris–Jones and Kothari, as discussed in this chapter, underemphasized some aspects of the party system as it prevailed in the 1960s. Thus, the party's influence remained relatively weak in many states, where it met with opposition or could not gain power or even when in power, was far from being dominant. Some Indian states which were less affected by the Congress's dominance and influence were the ex-princely states of Rajasthan, Madhya Pradesh, and Odisha, the northeastern states, as well as the relatively more politically mobilized states of Tamil Nadu, West Bengal, Punjab, and Kerala. Viewed from this perspective, the Congress system better represented a party system that existed at the national level rather than the overall Indian party system (Yadav and Palshikar 2006).

In summary, the Congress system was a consequence of the specific set of circumstances in which the party was formed before India's Independence, and how the electoral politics evolved thereafter. It was a unique, 'ideal-type' representation of a one-party-dominated system, which existed alongside the democratic functioning of the parliament, and sustained itself due to the legitimacy it gained from leading the Independence struggle, Congress's leadership, a centrist consensus, as well as important organizational and patronage advantages. Over time, Congress's dominance receded due to the weakening of these factors and the emergence of a more united opposition, producing a more fragmented and competitive party system. This also created electoral space for the regional parties, as well as the BJP that emerged as a challenger to the Congress at the national and the state levels.

3

Hindu Nationalism and Rise of the BJP

The BJP was formed in 1980 and is seen as a Hindu nationalist party. It won only two seats in the 1984 national election, but grew to emerge as the single largest party in the 1999 election winning 182 seats, and formed the BJP-led National Democratic Alliance (NDA) coalition government. It also expanded its political footprint in the 1990s by winning assembly elections in many states, especially in the northern Hindi-speaking and western parts of the country. It won a decisive victory in the latest national election held in 2014, having achieved a majority of seats on its own, followed this success by winning many state assembly elections, and has now emerged as the principal national party of the country.

Hindu Nationalism as a Political Ideology

In general, Hindu nationalism is based on the ideology of 'Hindutva', which refers to India's nationhood being based on Hindu cultural practices and traditions. Varshney (2013) refers to two alternative versions of Indian nationhood, which have been in contestation in India since the 1920s: secular nationalism and Hindu nationalism. Secular nationalism views all religions as equal and was the Congress party's ideological theme in its fight against the British colonial rule. Later, it formed the basis for the type of secularism adopted in the Indian Constitution despite a large majority of the country's population following Hinduism. Hindu nationalism, on the other hand, stresses on India being a Hindu nation, acceptance of Hindu dominance, and assimilation of religious minorities. Thus, while secular nationalism promotes social and religious diversity and a 'salad bowl' view of the Indian nation, Hindu nationalism favours the 'melting pot' view as a means of achieving social cohesion in the country (Varshney, 2013).

Although Hindu nationalism as a political ideology became prominent in the 1920s, its roots were in the various religious reformist movements of the nineteenth century. For example, the Arya Samaj, which was founded in 1875 in western India, stressed the reformation of orthodox Hindu religious practices, opposed idol worship, caste restrictions and untouchability, and had an anti-Muslim orientation. It called for the use of Hindi language (in the Devanagari script), rather than Urdu (using Arabic script), to be used for official purposes in India. To counter the Hindu reformist movements, societies for defending Hindu orthodoxy emerged in the form of Sanatan Dharam sabhas towards the end of the nineteenth century.

In the early twentieth century, Hindu sabhas were formed by the Arya Samajis and the Sanatanis in many Indian provinces in reaction to the announcement of separate electorates for the Muslims in the imperial and local legislative councils by the British in 1906. These organizations later united under the umbrella organization the All India Hindu Mahasabha or the Hindu Mahasabha in 1915. It had an anti-Muslim stance, undertook *shuddhi* or purification programmes aimed at abolishing untouchability, and was relaunched in the 1920s adopting a more active political role. The Hindu Mahasabha was not a separate political party, but functioned like a subgroup of the Congress. However, with the rising influence of Gandhi in the Congress and his stress on a broad-based brand of politics, the Hindu Mahasabha delinked itself from the Congress and became a separate political party in the late 1930s (Jaffrelot 2010: 44–5).

Hindu nationalism as a political ideology became more prominent when V.D. Savarkar took over as the president of the Hindu Mahasabha in 1937. Under Savarkar, the organization's ideology became more radical, and it was viewed by Congress leaders as a communal and a Hindu fundamentalist party. Savarkar's 'Hindutva' doctrine became the centre point of Hindu nationalism, and was based around religion, language, and the sacred land (Hindu, Hindi, Hindustan). According to him, a Hindu is one who lives in Hindustan, the sacred land beyond the Indus, between the Himalayas and the Indian Ocean. Further, as Hindus formed the majority and were the autochthonous people of India, all minorities were considered as outsiders who needed to adhere to Hindutva culture and pay allegiance to Hindu symbols (Jaffrelot 2010: 45). And therefore, only those who viewed India as their 'fatherland' and 'holyland' belonged to the Hindu nation. As a political organization, the Hindu Mahasabha was pushed to the political margins after the 1937 provincial elections during the British colonial rule. Although Savarkar's leadership and his idea of Hindutva transformed the Hindu Mahasabha into a Right-wing, Hindu, communalist, political alternative to the Congress, the party could not achieve electoral success and suffered defeats in the 1946 provincial elections.

The RSS and the BJS

The RSS, a Right-wing Hindu cultural organization, was formed in 1925 in Nagpur by K.B. Hedgewar, who was its first head or *sarsanghchalak*. Ideologically, the RSS called upon the religious minorities, especially the Muslims, to pledge allegiance to Hindu symbols and culture. Jaffrelot (2010: 38) notes that the RSS was formed soon after the formation of the CPI and before the first socialist party in India, and that Hindu nationalism ran parallel to the transformation of the Congress into a mass organization. The RSS inculcated martial values amongst its members through physical and ideological training to fulfil its main objectives of propagating the Hindutva ideology. Although the RSS became the most powerful Hindu nationalist organization, it largely remained cultural and apolitical, especially under M.S. Golwalkar as its second Sarsanghchalak.

In 1948, just a few months after India's Independence, Mahatma Gandhi was assassinated by Nathuram Godse, a Hindu Brahmin. Although the RSS was not directly involved in the assassination (Guha 2007: 98), it led to a backlash against the Hindu Mahasabha and the RSS. As a result, the Hindu Mahasabha became marginalized, and the RSS was banned. A new Hindu nationalist political party, the BJS, was formed in 1951 by some prominent members of the Hindu Mahasabha (Mahasabhites) led by S.P. Mookerjee with the support of the RSS after the ban on it was lifted in 1949, as the Hindu nationalists wanted to strengthen their political influence.

The BJS emerged as the most prominent Hindu nationalist party after the 1952 national election, and this led to the absorption of many members of the Hindu Mahasabha into the BJS. The party positioned itself as a Right-wing nationalist party that stressed Hindu traditions, emphasized the need for a Hindu *sangathan* (the organization of the Hindu community), an *akhand* Bharat ('an undivided India', including Pakistan), advocated Hindi to be adopted as India's national language, called for the abolition of cow-slaughter, and favoured taking a strong line with Pakistan (Graham 1987). The party was also against providing concessions to religious minorities, especially Muslims, creation of linguistic states, and granting of autonomous status to the Muslim-dominated state of Jammu and Kashmir (Jaffrelot 2013). Politically, it opposed the Congress as well as the Communists. In the 1950s and early 1960s, the Hindu nationalists, including the BJS, did not actively politicize religion as a cleavage. As Jaffrelot (2013) points out, Nehru's commitment to secularism was an important factor that contained the most extreme use of religion by Hindu nationalists. However, after Nehru's death, the tolerance for other religions became a matter of political calculation rather than of principle (Desai 2009: 298).

Like the RSS, the BJS followed activist values of Hindu nationalism. The functioning and organization of the BJS also resembled the RSS structure of a disciplined hierarchy, based around the *shakhas* (local branches). The party was also reliant on the RSS for support and membership. Following the death of S.P. Mookerjee in 1953, the RSS was able to exert a stronger influence over the BJS. However, the popularity of the BJS remained limited to traditional, upper-caste elites of north India—the Brahmins and Banias—in its initial years, and it was perceived as a niche party less interested in winning elections than in using these to propagate its Hindu nationalist ideology. This strategy, however, acted as a deterrent to its growth and political influence.

Many other social and religious organizations affiliated to the RSS were formed between 1940 and 1960, which together constitute the Sangh Parivar or the family of the Sangh (the RSS). The Vishwa Hindu

Parishad (VHP) or the World Council of Hindus was the most prominent of these organizations, which aimed at providing a centralized structure to organize Hindu religion, and was supported in its efforts by its militant youth wing, the Bajrang Dal. Although these organizations were not political parties, they worked to promote the interests and philosophy of the RSS and Hindu nationalism in their respective spheres of influence.

Electoral Performance of the BJS

In the 1952 national election, the BJS won just 3 (0.6 per cent) seats and 3.1 per cent of the votes, but was recognized as one of the four national parties by the ECI. The party improved its performance in subsequent elections, winning 4 (0.8 per cent) seats with 5.9 per cent vote share in 1957 and 14 (2.8 per cent) seats with 6.4 per cent vote share in 1962 (Table 3.1). Its performance peaked in the 1967 national election, when it won 35 (6.7 per cent) seats with a 9.3 per cent vote share. The party also improved its performance in the state assembly elections, so that by the late 1960s, it became the ruling party or the dominant element in non-Congress coalition governments in many states. In the 1971 national election, its last as a separate party before merging into Janata Party, the BJS won 22 (4.2 per cent) seats with a 7.3 per cent vote share.

TABLE 3.1 Performance of the BJS in National Elections (Lok Sabha), 1952–71

	1952	1957	1962	1967	1971
Number of seats contested	94	130	196	249	157
Number of seats won	3	4	14	35	22
Seat share (%)	0.6	0.8	2.8	6.7	4.2
Vote share (%)	3.1	5.9	6.4	9.3	7.3

Source: Collated by the author based on ECI election statistics.

After the 1969 split in the Congress, the BJS formed alliances with anti-Congress opposition parties in 1971, in order to replace Congress (R), the Congress faction led by Indira Gandhi. The BJS only won 22 seats in the 1971 national election, which was 13 seats less than it won in 1967. The Congress won the majority of seats, and also won back many states in the 1971 and 1972 assembly elections, where the BJS had performed well in 1967. Thereafter, the BJS adopted a more centrist strategy, softening the party's line on Hindu nationalism and toning down its earlier support for Hindi language. It also became supportive of the 'JP movement', the anti-Congress, anti-Indira movement under the leadership of J.P. Narayan, a former Congress member and a socialist leader.

The national emergency declared by Indira Gandhi in June 1975 was lifted in 1977 with the declaration of a new election. It led to the anti-Congress parties, including the BJS, to amalgamate into the Janata Party, a united opposition front, to contest the 1977 national election under the party label BLD. The Janata Party comprised the Congress (O), the BJS, the BLD, the Socialist Party, and some Congress rebel factions, and had support from other parties such as the 'Congress for Democracy' (CFD) that was led by ex-Congress member Jagjivan Ram. This election saw an overwhelming victory for the Janata Party, which won 298 of the 542 seats in the Lok Sabha, with former members of the BJS winning over 90 of these seats, many of whom also became ministers in the new government. The former members of the BJS also formed the largest or dominant groups within the Janata governments formed in many states, for example, Madhya Pradesh, Himachal Pradesh, and Rajasthan, and some of them also became state chief ministers.

By 1979, the Janata Party was facing internal factionalism and many of its leaders left the party to form their own parties. For instance, Raj Narain formed the Secular Janata Party or Janata (S), claiming that it had no links with the communal forces such as the RSS, and many prominent Janata leaders like Charan Singh also joined this party later. In July 1979, Morarji Desai of the Janata Party resigned as the prime minister, leading to a political crisis that prompted the president of India to invite Charan Singh to form a government. Although Charan Singh took over as the prime minister, he had to rely on support from Congress (S), the anti-Indira faction of the Congress, as well as the Congress (I), the rebranded faction led by Indira Gandhi. Given the unstable nature of this coalition, Charan Singh's government fell within three months and a fresh national election was held in January 1980. Although the Janata Party government had collapsed, and the Janata Party split, the former members of the BJS decided to fight the 1980 election as part of the reduced Janata Party. However, the Congress under the leadership of Indira Gandhi won a landslide victory, and the rump Janata Party could only win 31 seats of which 14 were won by the former members of the BJS (Graham 1987).

The BJS came under increasing attack from within the Janata bloc on the dual membership issue—referring to complete delinking and dissociation of the BJS from the RSS, but the party continued to stay in the Janata Party. However, in March 1980, the Janata Party's national executive endorsed the decision that its members should have no links to the RSS. Following this, the BJS decided to form a new party in April 1980—the BJP.

Politicization of Hindu Nationalism and the Rise of the BJP

Although Hindu nationalism had arisen as a social, and later a political movement in the nineteenth and early twentieth century, a Hindu nationalist party could not emerge as a major political force until the BJP arrived on the scene in 1980. The lack of consolidation of the Hindu vote was despite Hinduism being prevalent in India since centuries, and with 80 per cent of the population following the Hindu religion in some form or the other. It is important to note that Hindus worship many gods, its practice is largely private and individualistic, and it lacks a single religious text, a hierarchical religious leadership, and a clear central authority. Viewed from this perspective, Hinduism is more like a 'conglomeration of sects' than a religion (Jaffrelot 2010: 40). Further, the lack of a single religious organization does not make Hinduism conducive to mass religious or political mobilization. The rise of a unified Hindu nationalist movement as a political force in India was also hampered by cross-cutting social cleavages of caste, language, and

77

region. As Seshia (1998) notes, a collective action problem caused by these cross-cutting cleavages led to only limited aggregation of the Hindu vote and hindered the assimilation of the Hindu fringe into the Hindu core.

Bose (2009) attributes the politicization of Hindu identity in India in the 1980s to the institutional practice of secularism and the processes of modernization. In particular, she argues that Hindu nationalism emerged as a powerful force by exploiting the perception of threat exhibited by the dominant Hindu community, and was able to adapt to the processes of modernization, making the Hindu religion more relevant to capitalist modernity. This, in turn, strengthened its appeal to a growing Hindu middle class, which favoured the country's integration into the global economy. The general erosion of democratic procedures within the Congress party, especially under Indira Gandhi, and the party's declining influence also created a political space that allowed the BJP to rise as a credible force in Indian politics. As Varshney (1993) argues, the Congress party's deterioration, especially under Indira Gandhi, led to an ideological vacuum in Indian politics which parties such as the BJP could exploit to further their ideology. The BJP's growth was also facilitated by its relatively cohesive ideology as well as by having a strong and disciplined cadre.

BJP's Growth and Electoral Performance

The BJP was formed in April 1980, and has its roots in the BJS that was formed in 1951 on a Right-wing Hindu nationalist agenda. At its inception, the BJP, under the leadership of A.B. Vajpayee and L.K. Advani, decided to be more moderate than its predecessor, and adopted the 'Five Commitments'. It was based on the principles of nationalism and national integration, commitment to democracy and fundamental rights, positive secularism that meant *sarva dharma sambhava* (all religions are equal), Gandhian socialism, and value-based politics (Graham 2006). These principles, especially Gandhian socialism, found opposition from some prominent leaders within the BJP as it stood in contrast to the opposition of the BJS to special rights for the minorities, and appeared more in line with the communist agenda and the Congress's ideals under Nehru. Although BJP retained ties with the RSS and its Hindu orientation, it aimed to become more centrist in its appeal, and attractive to a wider electorate. The party also adopted a new party symbol and flag, and decided not to use Jana Sangh as its party label.

Since its formation in 1980, the BJP has grown dramatically with respect to its electoral performance (Table 3.2). From winning just two seats in the 1984 national election, BJP's seat tally rose to 85 in 1989,

120 in 1991, and 161 in 1996, when it first emerged as the single largest party. Its success continued in the 1998 and 1999 national elections when it won 182 seats on both occasions, and was able to lead the NDA coalition governments. Although the BJP-led NDA lost the 2004 and 2009 national elections to the Congress-led UPA coalition and the BJP's seat and vote share declined, it returned to power through a decisive victory in the 2014 national election, winning a majority of seats (282) on its own, the first time any single party was able to do so since the 1984 election.

The BJP fought its first national election in 1984 with a moderated stand on Hindu nationalism, on a manifesto that emphasized issues such as national unity, poverty, electoral reforms, and 'positive secularism' that stressed protection of the minorities. However, it could win only two seats and 8 per cent of votes, while the Congress won a landslide victory. This defeat prompted the BJP leadership to rethink their strategy to transform the party into a mass-based organization. The BJP's leadership changed, as L.K. Advani took over as the new party president from A.B. Vajpayee in 1986. Advani inducted four new party general secretaries, all with an RSS background, thus restoring the party's close ties with the RSS.

The Shah Bano controversy in 1985 gave a fillip to the BJP's Hindu nationalist agenda. Shah Bano, a

TABLE 3.2 BJP's Performance in National Elections (Lok Sabha), 1984–2014

	1984	1989	1991	1996	1998	1999	2004	2009	2014
Number of seats contested	224	225	468	471	388	339	364	433	428
Number of seats won	2	85	120	161	182	182	138	116	282
Seat share (%)	0.4	16	23	30	34	34	25	21	52
Vote share (%)	8	11	20	20	26	24	22	19	31

Source: Collated by the author based on ECI election statistics.

Muslim divorcee woman, was granted maintenance rights by the Supreme Court of India, which went against the Muslim Personal Law, and angered the orthodox Muslim clergy. The Congress government superseded the court's judgment by passing a law, which prompted the BJP to call Congress 'pseudo-secular', and pass a resolution in 1986 which condemned this as a retrograde step and a move against the directive principles of the Indian Constitution that require the state to move towards adopting a uniform civil code. As BJP's president, Advani focused on the issues of Hindu nationalism, banning cow slaughter, abrogating the special status given to the state of Jammu and Kashmir under Article 370 of the Constitution, and the introduction of a uniform civil code.

For the 1989 national election, the BJP decided to engage in seat-sharing and joint-campaigning arrangement with the JD, and highlighted corruption under the Congress government as the main election issue. The JD won 141 seats and BJP 85 (with an 11 per cent vote share). The NF coalition of opposition parties formed the government, which the BJP decided not to join, but support from outside. The NF government decided to implement the Mandal Commission Report that recommended 27 per cent reservation of jobs in government organizations and seats in higher educational institutions for the 'OBC'. There were violent protests, especially from upper-caste Hindu youth, against this reservation policy, and in an attempt to create unity among the Hindus in light of the Mandal decision, Advani launched a rath yatra (chariot procession) from Somnath in Gujarat to Ayodhya in Uttar Pradesh.

This brought to the forefront the issue of building a mandir (temple) at Ayodhya, believed to be the Hindu god Lord Ram's *janmabhoomi* (birthplace), which had allegedly been destroyed by Muslim invaders and replaced by the Babri Masjid. Advani was arrested in Bihar en route to Ayodhya, at the order of Bihar's chief minister, Lalu Prasad Yadav of the JD, on the grounds of stirring communal tensions. The BJP then withdrew support from the NF government and it fell in 1990. The Ram Mandir issue also formed part of the BJP's 1991 national election manifesto, and this indicated their return to a more radical brand of religious politics—*Mandal* (caste-based reservations issue) versus *Kamandal* (a symbol of Hinduism), and the party contested various state assembly elections during 1989–91 using a communally polarized platform.

This strategy arguably helped the BJP to improve its electoral performance and emerge as the second largest party in the 1991 national election, winning 120 (23 per cent) seats with a vote share of 20 per cent, although the Congress emerged as the single largest party, winning 232 seats. The electoral support for the BJP came mainly from the Hindi-speaking areas (Hindi belt) in north and central India. In the Uttar Pradesh state assembly election held in 1991, BJP emerged as the winner with a majority of seats (221 as opposed to 57 seats in 1989), and a vote share of 31 per cent (compared to 18 per cent in 1989). The BJP formed the state government, and this success was largely attributed to the Ram Mandir agenda of the party. During 1989–91, the party also achieved victories in the state assembly elections in Gujarat, Himachal Pradesh, Madhya Pradesh, and Rajasthan, and also made significant gains in its vote share in other states such as Bihar and Maharashtra. The BJP's success continued with it forming governments in many states on its own or as part of coalitions in the 1990s.

M.M. Joshi took over as the BJP's president in 1991, and undertook a rath yatra, called the Ekta Yatra (a journey for unity), to highlight the issue of Kashmiri Hindus who had been displaced from their home state of Jammu and Kashmir. The issue of Ram Mandir picked up further momentum, which culminated in the demolition of Babri Masjid by Hindu nationalist militants in December 1992. Following this, the BJP governments in the states of Uttar Pradesh, Madhya Pradesh, Rajasthan, and Himachal Pradesh were dismissed by the Congress government at the centre.

Advani took over as the party president again in 1993. During this period, the BJP was perceived as a party largely based on the issue of Hindutva with a focus on Ram Mandir, and the party realized that it needed to expand its electoral appeal beyond this issue if it wanted to come to power at the national level.

Just before the 1996 national election, Advani, considered as a hard-line Hindu nationalist, announced that Vajpayee, a moderate, would be BJP's prime ministerial candidate. The party fought this election mainly focusing on the failures and bribery charges against the Congress government rather than solely on a Hindutva agenda. It emerged as the largest party in the Lok Sabha, winning 161 seats with a 20 per cent vote share, despite the Congress winning a higher vote share of 28 per cent, but a lower number of seats at 140. Although the BJP was invited to form the government, it was unable to garner the required support to forge a majority, and Vajpayee resigned from the post of the prime minister just 13 days after assuming office. Most of the BJP's seats in this election came from the states of Uttar Pradesh and Madhya Pradesh, and this showed the limitations of BJP expanding into other states without electoral alliances with other parties.

The 1998 national election saw the BJP shelving its Hindutva agenda, and adopting a more moderate plank in order to form electoral alliances with other parties, a strategy that had also helped it to win many state assembly elections and make inroads into states such as West Bengal and Odisha. Along with its geographical expansion, the BJP also succeeded in expanding its social base amongst the lower castes and classes in some states (Thachil 2014). Once again, the BJP emerged as the party with the largest number (182) of seats with a 25 per cent vote share, while the Congress secured a higher vote share of 26 per cent, but a lower number of seats at 141. Vajpayee was sworn in as the prime minister for the second time, and led the NDA coalition consisting of a large number of ideologically diverse parties. However, his government fell after about 18 months in power when an alliance partner, the AIADMK, withdrew from the coalition.

The BJP continued its strategy of making alliances in a more systematic manner for the 1999 national election. This election took place against the backdrop of a conflict between India and Pakistan in the Kargil region of Kashmir, which ended with the Pakistan government ordering its troops to withdraw from the region. This gave rise to a surge of patriotic fervour in India, which benefited the BJP. This election saw the incumbent BJP-led NDA getting a parliamentary majority, winning 298 of 543 seats with a vote share of 41 per cent, with BJP's seat tally being 182. Vajpayee was sworn in as the prime minister for the third time.

The results of the 1999 election highlighted the importance of establishing strategic electoral alliances with other regional and caste-based parties by the BJP. The party continued its electoral success in large Hindi-speaking states, for example, Bihar and Uttar Pradesh, but failed to win seats in the southern states, with the exception of Karnataka and Tamil Nadu. The BJP-led NDA coalition included 14 allies working around a common policy programme, the National Agenda, and lasted its full electoral term, the first time in the history of independent India that a large coalition of diverse parties had done so.

The BJP's expansion during the period 1989–2004 took place in three overlapping stages (Sridharan 2005). In the first stage, the BJP sought to gain support in specific geographical regions consisting of several state assembly and some Lok Sabha constituencies. The party then worked towards displacing or becoming the main challenger to the Congress in states such as Rajasthan, Madhya Pradesh, and Gujarat. The third stage saw the BJP engaging in active coalition strategy, particularly after 1996, to expand into states where it had relative limited influence within the Hindi belt and Gujarat, in the southern and the eastern states. Thus, the basic driver of BJP's coalition strategy was to gain bridging votes to win a plurality, and it aggressively pursued electoral alliances or seat adjustments with

potential allies, often ignoring ideological incompat-
ibilities. And thus, the strategic exploitation of coalition
opportunities was a major factor in BJP's expansion
during 1998–2004, in addition to the appeal of its
Hindu nationalist ideology. The BJP's success during
the late 1990s and early 2000s has also been linked
to the provision of local services (mainly educational
and medical) provided privately through its affiliate
organizations, which helped the party to improve its
support amongst Dalits and tribals in specific parts
of the country (Thachil 2014). This service-based
approach was attractive because it was less threatening
to BJP's elite core than alternative approaches based on
redistributive shifts in policies or patronage.

The 2004 national election was called six months
early by the NDA government in light of the high
economic growth, and the party's own perception of
a general 'feel-good factor' in the country, which the
BJP highlighted in its 'India Shining' election campaign. Learning from the BJP's coalition strategy, the
Congress, too, formed the United Progressive Alliance
(UPA) with many regional parties. However, the BJP
suffered an unexpected defeat, and its 'India Shining'
slogan backfired. The party received a lower percentage (22 per cent) of the votes and 138 seats (compared
to 182 seats in 1999). The NDA's seat tally was also
reduced by almost a third of its seats, from 298 seats in

1999 to 189 in 2004. The Congress, on the other hand, gained from following a coalition strategy. Together with its allies, it won 222 seats, and formed a UPA coalition government with the outside support of the Left parties (the CPI and CPM) and the BSP, and later, the SP. Sonia Gandhi, the widow of former Congress president, Rajiv Gandhi, decided not to become the prime minister, and instead, the party decided that Manmohan Singh, who was the finance minister in the Congress government during 1991–6, would lead the UPA government.

The 2009 national election was largely a repeat of the 2004 election, fought between the two rival coalition blocs—the UPA and the NDA—and saw both the Congress and the BJP continuing their strategies of making alliances, although many of the BJP's allies decided to leave the NDA. The BJP's campaign was led by L.K. Advani, and focused on security issues and bringing back Indian money illegally stashed abroad. The UPA returned to power with an increased tally of 262 seats while the NDA's seats fell to 159. After BJP's election defeats in 2004 and 2009, there were speculations that the party may return to a more radical electoral agenda focused on Hindutva.

According to Jaffrelot (2013), whether the BJP and its predecessor the BJS pursued a path of radicalization or that of moderation in their efforts to grow as a national party has been influenced by its relationship with the RSS, the perception of the Muslim community prevailing at a given time as well as the electoral strategies of the other competing parties. Further, during the BJP's trajectory of growth, the judgement about politicizing religion to organize the party and use of Hindutva as a political strategy has been debated within the party. While some BJP leaders have argued that a narrow focus on Hindutva will not help the party to occupy a dominant position in Indian politics, others within the party and the RSS have called for the party to become a more Hindu-centric party.

For the 2014 national election, the BJP projected Narendra Modi as a charismatic leader and its prime ministerial candidate, who had risen from humble origins to become the chief minister of the state of Gujarat, and who was credited by many for effective governance and economic development in the state. However, he was also considered a controversial figure for his alleged role in the communal riots of 2002 in Gujarat. Although a Supreme Court inquiry cleared Modi of these charges, his critics continued to question his role in the handling of these riots during the 2014 election campaign. The BJP's election strategy in 2014 was that of moderation, and focused on effective governance, decisive leadership, inclusive development, and the Congress's corruption, while avoiding the contentious issues of Ram Mandir, uniform civil code, and abrogation of Article 370. Modi's slogans of 'Toilets Over Temples' and '*Achche Din Ayenge*' (Good days are ahead) stressed the BJP's promise of economic development for all.

The BJP won 282 seats, a gain of 166 seats, with a vote share of 31 per cent, representing its highest seat and vote share since the party's formation in 1980. It was also the first time that a non-Congress party achieved a majority on its own since 1977, when the Janata Party won the election, which was the biggest win by any single party since the 1984 election. The Congress slipped to its worst-ever performance in a national election, winning just 44 seats. The BJP's victory prompted some commentators to call 2014 a 'critical election', where it had become a 'dominant party' like the Congress of the 1950s and 1960s. Even so, to sustain its success, the BJP faces challenges to expand its footprint, especially in the southern and the eastern parts of the country, and also to reach out more strategically to minorities. Whether the BJP will become the system-defining party in India will be determined by the balance it is able to strike between highlighting Hindutva as its main political agenda, and exploiting more socially inclusive electoral strategies.

The decline of the Congress in the late 1980s created a political space that allowed the BJP's rise as a credible political force in Indian politics. Although the BJP, like its predecessor the BJS, has followed the Hindutva agenda, the party's electoral strategies have varied depending on electoral competition and demands of the political environment. In the 1990s, the BJP was seen as a party largely driven by a religious nationalist ideology, and was traditionally associated with prosperous upper-caste Hindus, mainly from states in north India. Since then, the party has adopted a more moderate image in order to forge electoral alliances, and has won support from a wider cross section of the electorate. However, Bose (2009) points out that if Hindu nationalism is able to find new ways of exploiting the anxieties, insecurities, and possibilities created by modernization, it will continue to play a prominent role in Indian politics. Similarly, Palshikar (2015a) argues that the possibility of the BJP transforming into a centrist party is low due to a combination of factors including the mixing of Hindutva identity with the development agenda, the covert pursuit of Hindutva by both the party and the BJP government, the deep-rooted relationship between Hindutva and the BJP, and the slow and imperceptible shifting of the middle ground of public opinion in India in favour of majoritarian (and therefore pro-Hindutva) sentiment.

The BJP's rise demonstrates that sociological factors continue to be important in shaping the Indian party system, as the party gained from politicizing the social cleavage of religion. It also shows that the BJP benefitted from building pre-poll electoral alliances and seat-sharing arrangements with other parties which, in the context of India's electoral system (SMPS), helped it increase its share of seats. A strong anti-incumbency sentiment against the UPA government, which faced allegations of corruption, as well as Modi's image of being an effective leader proved to be important contextual factors behind the BJP's victory in 2014. The fact that this victory was achieved on the basis of the lowest ever vote share of a party winning a majority, also illustrated the continuing importance of institutional arrangements, especially electoral rules, as an important determinant of the party system in India.

The BJP's growth in the late 1980s and 1990s coincided with the establishment and growth of many regional parties in India, which in conjunction with the continuing decline of the Congress led to a new phase of fragmentation of the Indian party system. This, in turn, brought new challenges for the national parties to work within the constraints of coalition settings, as well as opportunities for the regional parties to share power and influence policy at the national level.

4

Fragmentation of the Party System and Coalition Politics

The party system in India at the national level in the post-1989 period has been characterized by fragmentation. The Congress is no longer the centre of the political scene, and the BJP has grown to become the principal national party. This phase also witnessed the rise of regional parties, which mainly appeal to voters based on identity politics, highlighting factors such as caste and regional affiliations. Due to the fragmentation of the party system, parties have found it difficult to achieve legislative majority at the centre, which has led to the need to forge electoral alliances to gain power. Coalition governments have therefore become the norm rather than the exception at the centre, and are also common in many states. In the seven national elections held between 1989 and 2009, India witnessed minority or coalition governments comprising a large number of ideologically heterogeneous parties, often with the outside support of other parties. As a result, many of these governments were not able to complete their full term, largely due to internal factionalism and withdrawal of support from coalition partners.

In this scenario, smaller parties have held disproportionate power in negotiating cabinet berths and influencing policy agenda, and have often been pivotal to the survival of coalition governments. This pivotality has, in turn, prompted parties to change affiliations for opportunistic reasons rather than based on ideology, leading to further fragmentation of the party system. Although the BJP was able to win majority of seats in the 2014 national election, the party system remains fragmented, and the need to build alliances continues to be crucial for parties in this diffused political environment.

The Size of the Indian Party System

The size of the party system or the number of parties competing in the electoral space is a useful measure to assess the degree of fragmentation of a party system. Empirically, the number of parties in an electoral competition space can be measured in actual (contesting) or effective terms (ENP) weighed by their respective share of votes or seats. Table 4.1 shows that on both these criteria, constituencies in Indian national elections typically witness competition between more than two parties. Therefore, India does not strictly follow Duverger's law, which predicts a two-party competition under SMPS. The average number of parties contesting elections at the constituency level increased from 5.8 during 1952–84 to 13.9 in the fragmentation phase during 1989–2014. The average ENP (by votes) has also remained well above 2 since India's first national election and increased to 2.8 during the phase of party fragmentation.

The pattern of party competition in India at the constituency level can be seen more clearly in a Nagayama diagram or triangle (Diwakar 2007), which plots the vote share of the winning party against that of the runner-up party. The left corner area of the triangle corresponds to the presence of multiple contesting parties, while the right corner represents single- or two-party dominance. The peak of the triangle reflects a two-party competition with limited third-party strength. Grofman et al. (2004) provide additional labelling of segments of the Nagayama triangle to facilitate visual comparison of the type of party competition. Based on this segmentation, constituencies located in areas A, B, and C generally represent a two-party competition, while those in areas F, G, and H represent

TABLE 4.1 Size of the Indian Party System at the Constituency Level (Lok Sabha), 1952–2014

					Phase of party fragmentation, 1989–2014					
	1952–84	1989	1991	1996	1998	1999	2004	2009	2014	1989–2014
Average number of contesting parties	5.8	11.6	16.3	25.7	8.7	8.6	10.0	14.9	15.2	13.9
Average ENP (by votes)	2.5.	2.5	2.9	3.0	2.7	2.6	2.8	3.1	2.8	2.8
Number of constituency elections	3711	529	537	543	543	543	543	543	543	4324

Source: ECI election statistics and author's calculations.

Note: 1. Eighty-six constituencies in the 1952 election and 91 in the 1957 election were two-member constituencies. One constituency in 1952 was three-member. All constituencies thereafter have been single-member, where voters elect one winner per constituency. The data presented in Table 4.1 only relates to single-member constituencies.

multiparty competition (Figure 4.1). The remaining areas D and E indicate neither a strict two-party nor a multiparty competition.

Figures 4.1(a) and 4.1(b) plot Nagayama diagrams for all Lok Sabha constituency elections for the period 1952–84 and 1989–2014, respectively. As shown, a higher proportion of constituencies populate areas A+B+C during 1952–84 compared to 1989–2014, reflecting a larger number of constituencies following a multiparty competition during the phase of fragmentation. Figures 4.1(c) and 4.1(d) provide similar plots for the northern region and Hindi belt, which account for 45 per cent of all Lok Sabha constituencies. As can be seen, areas F+G+H are clearly more populated than areas A+B+C, evidencing that a large majority of the constituencies have witnessed a multiparty competition in these two regions. This points towards a higher level of party fragmentation in India at the constituency level.

Although the average ENP has remained above two at the constituency level despite the predictions of Duverger's law, this has to be contextualized in light of India's extreme social heterogeneity. Empirical studies have indicated that majoritarian systems limit the impact of ethnic and religious diversity on party system fragmentation. This constraining effect in the Indian context is denoted by a large number of contesting parties at the constituency level (averaging 13.9 during 1989–2014), but a relatively small ENP by votes (averaging 2.8), as is shown in Table 4.1. Chhibber and Murali (2006: 5) attribute the 'non-random' deviations from Duverger's law in the state assembly elections in India to the influence of federal arrangements, whereby more than two parties get votes in a constituency when either more than two national parties or a combination of national and regional parties compete in a state. As Diwakar (2007) argues, a comprehensive set of explanatory variables, including both institutional and sociological factors, are needed to explain the size of the Indian party system at the constituency level.

The trends at the national level provide a clearer picture of the fragmentation of the Indian party system. Table 4.2 shows that the number of contesting parties rose from an average of 35 in the pre-fragmentation phase to 234 thereafter. It also shows that although the ENP by seats averaged around two during 1952–84, confirming the dominance of the Congress, this measure increased substantially after 1989 as the party system fragmented, and stood at 6.5 in the 2004 election. In the next two elections, ENP by seats declined and was 3.5 in the 2014 election due to the BJP's exceptional victory. However, during the entire phase of party fragmentation during 1989–2014, the

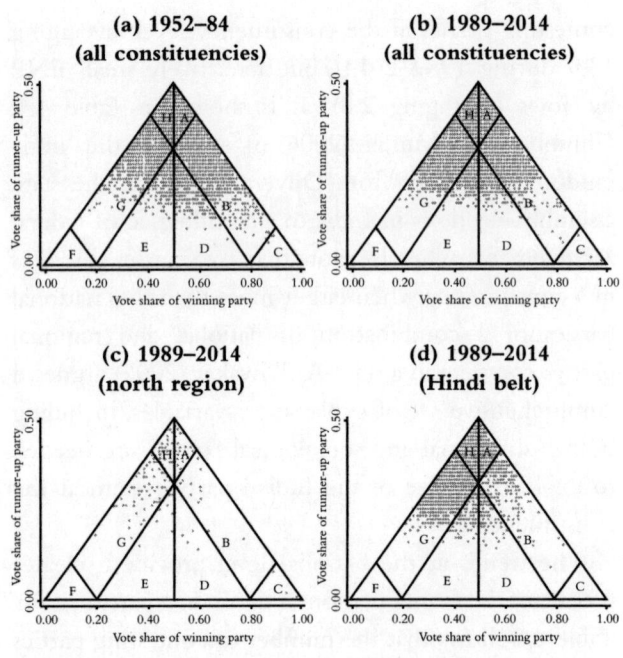

**(a) 1952–84
(all constituencies)**

**(b) 1989–2014
(all constituencies)**

**(c) 1989–2014
(north region)**

**(d) 1989–2014
(Hindi belt)**

FIGURE 4.1 Nagayama Diagram Showing Competition at the Constituency Level (Lok Sabha)

Source: Author's calculations based on ECI election statistics.

Notes: 1. Each point in the diagram represents a constituency election outcome as regards the vote share of the winning and the runner-up party; 2. Areas A+B+C indicate two-party competition, while F+G+H denote a multiparty competition. Areas D and E represent neither a strict two-party nor a multiparty competition; 3. 'North' region includes Punjab, Chandigarh, and Jammu and Kashmir; 'Hindi belt' includes Uttar Pradesh, Bihar, Jharkhand, Rajasthan, Uttarakhand, Haryana, Madhya Pradesh, Chhattisgarh, Delhi, and Himachal Pradesh.

average ENP by seats was 5.0, indicating proliferation of the number of parties getting seats in the Lok Sabha. Further, the average ENP by votes, arguably a better indicator of party system fragmentation, was 4.3 during 1952–84, but rose to 6.9 in the 2014 election, averaging 6.6 during the entire fragmentation phase. The number of parties that won seats in the Lok Sabha also doubled from an average of 19 in the pre-fragmentation phase to 38 in the 2014 election, averaging 33 during 1989–2014. Thus, based on standard measures, the Indian party system at the national level fragmented in the 1990s, with an increase in both the contesting parties and the ENP by seats and votes.

Although the size of the Indian party system at the constituency level has not deviated substantially from the predictions of the Duverger's law, especially when seen in the context of the high social diversity in India, the party system at the national level has seen competition between many parties, and a higher degree of fragmentation since the 1990s. Sridharan (2003) notes that there are two contradictory pulls on the size of the Indian party system: Duverger's law pulling towards bipolarization, and ethnic heterogeneity, combined with disillusioned voting, pulling in the direction of new parties.

While there are only two leading parties or coalitions competing in most Indian states, these differ from

TABLE 4.2 Size of the Indian Party System at the National Level (Lok Sabha), 1952–2014

| | 1952–84 | Phase of party fragmentation, 1989–2014 | | | | | | | 1989–2014 | 1952–2014 |
		1989	1991	1996	1998	1999	2004	2009	2014		
Number of contesting parties	35	113	145	209	176	169	230	363	464	234	134
Effective number of parties (by seats)	2.1	4.1	3.6	5.8	5.4	6.1	6.5	5.0	3.5	5.0	3.6
Effective number of parties (by votes)	4.3	4.8	5.1	7.1	6.9	6.7	7.6	7.6	6.9	6.6	5.5
Number of parties in the Lok Sabha	19	24	24	28	39	38	38	37	38	33	26

Source: Author's calculations based on ECI election statistics.

state to state, which has led to a large number of parties at the national level. The formation of national party system in a polity involves coordination by voters and parties across the country's electoral districts and geography. Thus, a national party system is affected by the strength of the 'aggregation' or 'linkage' between the national and constituency-level party systems. Chhibber and Kollman (2004) stress the importance of centralization and decentralization on the degree of party aggregation, and argue that fiscal decentralization in India in the early 1990s led to the growth of regional parties and the consequent fragmentation of the party system at the national level. Extending this argument further, Diwakar (2010) suggests that the state-level party system is an intermediate level between the national and the constituency levels that can affect the party aggregation phenomenon, and shows that the 'dependence of states' for resources on the central government is an important determinant of the level of party aggregation at the state level. Schakel and Swenden (2016: 20) confirm the gradual decrease in the nationalization (aggregation) of the Indian party system, and identify a decline in 'electorate congruence', or the extent to which state electorates diverge from each other in elections, as being the main reason for this phenomenon.

In a highly nationalized system, the nature of party competition in all constituencies is similar, and the ENP at the national level should be close to the average ENP across the country's constituencies. Figure 4.2 shows that while the average ENP (by votes) in the Indian constituencies has remained relatively stable, the ENP at the national level has increased significantly, indicating the inability of national parties to aggregate support across the country, leading to a fragmented party system. This shows that the fragmentation of the Indian party system has occurred because of the diversity of parties contesting elections in different parts of the country rather than a significant increase in the number of parties that compete at the constituency level. This, in turn, has been caused by the rise of many regional parties, which compete and have been successful in one or few states.

The Rise of Regional Parties

The period following the 1967 national election in India saw the emergence of anti-Congress alliances for both the national and the state assembly elections. According to Sridharan (2002), this phase witnessed a bipolar consolidation, where there was a strengthening of the non-Congress opposition, with the Congress being displaced as one of the two leading parties or

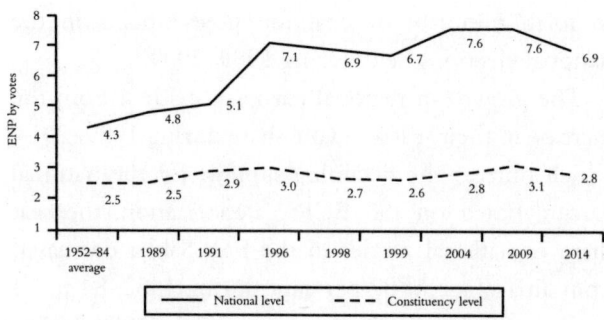

FIGURE 4.2 Effective Number of Parties (By Votes), 1952–2014
Source: Author's calculations based on ECI election statistics.

part of coalitions in many states. And this became a driving force for the fragmentation of the national party system after 1989 and has been described by Yadav (1999) as India's 'third electoral system', where many dormant social identities such as caste became politically salient. As a result, major national parties lost support in the late 1980s and the 1990s in many states to regional parties, for example, the SP and BSP in Uttar Pradesh, TDP in Andhra Pradesh, SHS and NCP in Maharashtra, AITC in West Bengal, RJD in Bihar, and BJD in Odisha. This led to an inability of the national parties to gain a majority in the Lok Sabha, and they had to increasingly rely on regional parties to form minority or coalition governments in the national elections held during 1989–2009.

The growth of regional parties is evident from the increase in their seat and vote share during 1989–2014, which mirrors the declining support for the national parties. Based on the ECI's categorization, the seat share of national parties in the Lok Sabha decreased from an average of 87 per cent during 1952–84 to 74 per cent in the phase of fragmentation (1989–2014), while that of state and other parties (mainly regional parties) increased from 13 per cent to 26 per cent (Table 4.3). Similar trends can be seen in vote share, where the share of votes of national parties decreased by 10 per cent during the phase of party fragmentation, while that of state and other parties increased by the same percentage. The actual number of state and other parties winning seats in the Lok Sabha also went up from an average of 18 in 1952–84, to 32 thereafter, as the party system fragmented.

Due to the fragmentation of the Indian party system, the combined seat and vote share of the two main national parties, the Congress and the BJP, averaged 58 per cent and 51 per cent, respectively, in 1989–2014, while that of other (mainly regional) parties accounted for a sizeable 42 per cent and 49 per cent of the seats and votes, respectively (Table 4.4).

Table 4.3 Seat Share and Vote Share of National and State/Other Parties (Lok Sabha), 1952–2014

	1952–1984 Average	1989	1991	1996	1998	1999	2004	2009	2014	1989–2014 Average
Seat share (%)										
National parties	87	89	89	74	71	68	67	69	63	74
State/other parties	13	11	11	26	29	32	33	31	37	26
Vote share (%)										
National parties	79	79	81	69	68	67	63	64	61	69
State/other parties	21	21	19	31	32	33	37	36	39	31
Number of contesting parties										
National parties	7	8	9	8	7	7	6	7	6	7
State parties	18	20	27	30	30	40	36	34	39	32

Source: Author's calculations based on ECI election statistics.
Note: Categorization of parties is according to ECI's definition.

TABLE 4.4 Seat Share and Vote Share of the Congress, BJP, and Other Parties (Lok Sabha), 1989–2014

Parties	1989	1991	1996	1998	1999	2004	2009	2014	1989–2014 Average
Seat share (%)									
Congress	37	45	26	26	21	27	38	8	29
BJP	16	23	30	34	34	25	21	52	29
Subtotal Congress + BJP	53	68	56	60	55	52	59	60	58
Other parties	47	32	44	40	45	48	41	40	42
Total	100	100	100	100	100	100	100	100	100
Vote share (%)									
Congress	40	36	29	26	28	27	29	19	29
BJP	11	20	20	26	24	22	19	31	22
Subtotal Congress + BJP	51	56	49	52	52	49	48	50	51
Other parties	49	44	51	48	48	51	52	50	49
Total	100	100	100	100	100	100	100	100	100

Source: Author's calculations based on ECI election statistics.

Ziegfeld (2012) points out that party system fragmentation in the 1990s took a regional form with the formation of small regional parties rather than small national parties. This trend of 'regionalization' of the party system has also been linked with the deepening of democracy in India through the expansion of political participation in the post-Congress era, where voters became more politically assertive. At the same time, the parties faced greater anti-incumbency phenomenon and competition in elections leading to alternations between parties in power both at the state and national level. From 1999 onwards, a more stable system of national coalition governments with the BJP-led NDA and the Congress-led UPA alternating in power emerged at the national level, even as regional parties continued to be important, and the state level remained the principal arena of political contestation. Although regional parties have been successful in gaining a substantial share of votes and seats, many of them are dynastic and personalistic, and centred around a single charismatic leader. Their rise has also coincided with the emergence of a clientelistic style of politics in India with specific promises to voters of cash, goods in kind, jobs, infrastructure, and access to government services that by right ought to have been provided to all (Wilkinson 2007).

India needs both strong national and regional parties to sustain its federal and secular democracy. National parties provide a mechanism to represent a wide variety of views, and to resist a parochial attitude towards the country's future, and therefore their decline can lead to political instability and secessionist tendencies. Regional parties, on the other hand, represent the interests of specific geographic regions or social groups, and provide continuous competition and challenge to the national parties, which is essential for a healthy democracy.

Explanations for the Fragmentation of the Indian Party System

The politicization of the social cleavages of caste, region, and religion during the 1980s and 1990s, and the decline in the Congress's prospects both at the national and the state level were the main factors that led to the proliferation of parties in India. Although the presence of social cleavages does not axiomatically result into political groupings and parties, it is a necessary condition for these cleavages to become politicized as salient electoral issues. According to Tillin (2015), the fragmentation of the party system happened within the context of India moving to a post–Congress polity and a phase of minority or coalition govern-

110

ments at the centre, in which regional parties played an important role. These included parties like the SP in Uttar Pradesh and the RJD in Bihar that focused on mobilizing lower castes, especially the OBC, following the implementation of the Mandal Commission recommendations in the 1990s. The BSP continued to mobilize the Dalits, although its influence remained largely limited to Uttar Pradesh. Other regional parties that emerged and led the way to the fragmentation of the Indian party system were the factional offshoots of national parties, for example, the AITC in West Bengal, BJD in Odisha, NCP in Maharashtra, and JDU in Bihar. Thus, the emergence of the regional parties reflected the 'regionalization' of national parties and the party system, rather than a set of regionalist agendas (Palshikar 2012).

Sridharan (2002) has provided various competing explanations for the fragmentation of the Indian party system. The politicization of social cleavages along regional lines since the late 1960s led to the rise and/ or further consolidation of regional parties such as the DMK, AGP, and SAD. The institutional arrangement of decoupling of the national and state assembly elections after 1971 facilitated the strategies of forging alliances of the parties at the state and the national level, which improved the prospects of regional parties. Further, increasing political consciousness amongst the newly mobilized social groups, such as the Dalits and the OBC, and the rise of parties such as the BSP and SP, which formed around the interests of these groups, contributed to the fragmentation of the party system. The decline of the Congress's organization forced the regional and traditional groups to support the regional parties, and the increasing devolution of power to the states incentivized the parties to organize at the state level to capture power. Party fragmentation was also facilitated by the effect of SMPS, whereby different parties engaged in bipolar competition in different parts of the country leading to a fragmented party system at the national level.

The success of regional parties in India has also been linked to pervasive clientelism where elites (politicians), rather than voters, are responsible for determining whether the party system includes successful regional parties, and voters are relatively indifferent to the choice between national and regional parties (Ziegfeld 2016). According to this view, the conducive institutional setting in the form of political, fiscal, and horizontal (bicameral parliament) decentralization, relatively low electoral thresholds, single-member constituencies, and no cross-regional contestation laws contributed towards the establishment and success of regional parties in India. Similarly, Chandra (2004: 6) characterizes India as a 'patronage democracy', where 'elected officials have discretion in the implementation of laws allocating the jobs and services at the disposal of the state'.

Coalition Politics in India

Since 1989, India has seen 11 minority or coalition governments at the national level (Table 4.5), of which 8 have been minority coalitions, 2 single-party minority governments while 1 was a surplus majority coalition in which the largest party had the majority on its own. Many of these governments have not lasted their full term.

According to Chakrabarty (2014: 84), 'coalition was inevitable because of the basic shift that had occurred in Indian politics following the disintegration of the Congress system and the consolidation of alternative centres of power based on distinct socio–economic and political interests'. The roots of this coalition era became evident by the late 1980s. In 1987, V.P. Singh, who had been expelled from the Congress for dissidence, launched Jan Morcha or the People's Front, which later merged with two main sections of the Lok Dal and the remnants of the erstwhile Janata Party to form the JD in 1988. The JD became the rallying

TABLE 4.5 Coalition Governments in India at the National Level, 1989–2014

S. No.	Election	Year of formation	Government	Dynamics
1.	1989	1989	NF coalition	Supported by BJP/Left parties; BJP withdrew support in 1990
2.		1990	JD	Outside Congress support; Congress withdrew support after 3 months
3.	1991	1991	Congress	Outside support from various parties; gained majority status in 1993
4.	1996	1996	BJP-led coalition	Unable to prove majority
5.		1996	UF–I coalition	Outside support of Congress; Congress withdrew support
6.		1996	UF–II coalition	Outside support of Congress; Congress withdrew support
7.	1998	1998	BJP-led coalition	AIADMK withdrew support in 1999
8.	1999	1999	NDA–I coalition	Lasted full term
9.	2004	2004	UPA–I coalition	Outside support from Left parties; withdrew support in 2008, instead, supported by SP
10.	2009	2009	UPA–II coalition	TMC withdrew in 2012 and DMK in 2013, but lasted full term
11.	2014	2014	NDA–II coalition (BJP majority)	Currently in power

Source: Collated by the author.

point for the NF, a heterogeneous alliance of many regional parties including the AGP, TDP, DMK, and Congress(S).

The NF, an anti-Congress formation that engaged in seat–sharing adjustments with the BJP and the communist parties for the 1989 national election, was able to defeat the Congress and formed a coalition government with the outside support of the BJP and the communists. Sridharan (2003) notes that the NF reintroduced the concept of 'seat adjustments' first used in 1977 by the opposition against the Congress, where spatially compatible parties do not compete in each other's strongholds. However, the NF coalition government was not stable and soon fell due to ideological incompatibility with the BJP, and in the 1991 national election, the NF contested against both the BJP and the Congress. Congress leader Rajiv Gandhi was assassinated during an election rally in Tamil Nadu, which helped the Congress gain sympathy of the voters and win the highest number of seats. Although the Congress fell short of the majority mark, it managed to form a minority government in 1991, which attained majority in 1993, and lasted its full term.

The 1996 national election saw the United Front (UF), an alliance of 15 parties, including the JD, SP, the CPI, and CPM and other smaller Left parties, forming the government with the outside support of the Congress. This election marked an important milestone, and a move towards the regionalization of politics in India. Due to political differences with some of the coalition partners, the Congress withdrew its support from Deve Gowda, the then prime minister, and instead supported a UF faction led by I.K. Gujral. In November 1997, Congress again withdrew support from Gujral's government, and fresh national election was called in February 1998. Pai (1996) has called the national elections of 1989, 1991, and 1996 as critical elections, which marked a breakdown of the national consensus and the Congress system.

In the 1998 national election, the BJP emerged as the largest party, and with the help of its alliance partners and the support of regional parties, was able to lead a coalition government. But this coalition did not last long and lost the vote of confidence when it was deserted by one of its partners, the AIADMK. Pai (1998) notes that despite no party having gained a majority following the 1998 election, two political blocs—the Congress and the BJP—became visible within the regionalized multiparty system. Further, several regional parties regrouped around these blocs by forming pre-poll and post-poll alliances, determining the emerging shape of the national party system.

Overall, the period from 1989 to 1998 saw various anti–Congress, anti–BJP 'third-front' alliances, comprising mainly regional parties, forming national coalition governments, and also witnessed the progression of the BJP to a national force and the key challenger to the Congress. Despite not sharing a common ideology, the constituent regional parties of these coalitions came together with a vision to share political power at the national level, and were supported by major national parties to further their political interests. Thus, in 1989, the BJP supported the NF to keep the Congress out of power, while in 1996 and 1998, the Congress supported the UF to contain the BJP. Within a decade, the third front suffered a significant decline, mainly due to the worsening prospects of the JD (Chakrabarty 2014: 115), and as a result, by 1999, the possibility of a third-front national government coming to power diminished substantially.

In the 1999 national election, the BJP pursued a formal alliance-making strategy, emerged as the largest party, and led the NDA coalition government. In contrast to earlier attempts to form coalitions that were unstable and could not last their full term, the BJP-led NDA coalition was able to do so. The main reasons for its stability were that it was a surplus majority coalition comprising more parties than were necessary for a majority, and it had an agreed common policy programme, the National Agenda. By the end of 2003, the Congress also realized the importance of forming electoral coalitions, and formed the UPA with the support of various regional parties. The Congress unexpectedly emerged as the largest single party, and the UPA won the 2004 election, defeating the incumbent NDA, and formed a coalition government. The UPA also drew on a Common Minimum Programme (CMP) to steer the government through the ideological differences of its constituent parties.

The UPA repeated its success in the 2009 national election and defeated the NDA. It lasted its full term, reinforcing the stabilization of the coalition era, where two rival blocs led by the two main national parties, the Congress and the BJP, contested national elections to win power. The 2014 election, however, marked a break in this trend and saw a single party, the BJP, achieving a majority, the first time it happened since 1984. Although the BJP decided to form an NDA coalition government, this was a coalition of choice rather than compulsion, and to this extent the 2014 election was exceptional.

Coalition formation in India has involved both pre-poll and post-poll arrangements where parties engage in seat adjustments and alliances. These arrangements have largely been opportunistic, aimed at maximizing votes and gaining power rather than based on an ideological congruence. In particular, parties have sought alliance partners to compensate for their relative lack of support in specific geographies, and given the primacy of spatial compatibility, ideology has often been relegated while assembling coalitions. For example, in 1989–2004, the BJP used state-level coalitions, building electoral alliances to expand in those states where it was competitive but not strong enough to win seats on its own, to increase its strength in the Lok Sabha (Sridharan 2005).

Kailash (2014b) notes that coalitions in India have been characterized by the mutual accommodation by polity-wide parties (the coalition makers) and the single-state parties (forming the pool of coalitionable), but has also involved contestation about policies and issues between coalition partners. Sridharan (2014: 56–7) identifies three reasons that facilitate the formation of minority governments and/or large and ideologically heterogeneous coalitions in India. The first reason relates to an institutional feature whereby in the event of a hung parliament, governments only need to demonstrate that a majority does not oppose them rather than demonstrate a majority. Secondly, the pattern of party fragmentation into several single-state parties and, consequently, the incentives for pre-electoral coalitions favour the formation of large, multiparty governments. Lastly, he refers to a 'lock-in' character of the supporting parties in the legislative coalition due to state-level electoral interdependencies and national level rivalries between major national parties within the Indian federal structure of governance. Thus, for regional parties, the main political consideration when joining a national coalition continues to be the implications for state-level politics.

According to Ziegfeld (2012), the advent of coalition governments in 1989 brought about the growth of the regional parties, as it increased the incentives for opportunistic politicians to establish and join regional parties that became pivotal to government formation and survival at the national level. Further, most of the new regional parties were founded by already successful leaders, who were members of national parties, but had quit to form their own regional parties to maximize their political rewards, for example, in the form of important ministerial positions in coalition governments. According to this view, the relationship between the formation and continuation of coalitions, and the rise of regional parties can be described as a feedback loop in which coalition governments initially facilitated the rise of regional parties in the 1990s, only for the success of these parties to then enhance the prospects of coalition governments in the 2000s.

The smooth transition of one coalition government (the NDA) to another (the UPA), following the 2004 election, suggested that the post-Congress Indian polity had stabilized and become accustomed to coalition governments. The era of 'federal coalitions' at the centre can also be viewed as a power-sharing device, whereby multiple diversities—religious, caste, linguistic, cultural, and regional—have access to power at the national level (Arora et al. 2013). Although this has created an atmosphere of 'cooperative federalism', it has also led to policy impasse and government instability due to the bargaining and competing interests of the coalition partners. In this situation, the power of parties to make or break a coalition and influence a voting outcome is more relevant than their absolute level of representation in the parliament.

Most of the regional parties were successful in negotiating important ministerial portfolios in the coalition governments formed at the centre from 1989 to 2009, and often held a substantially higher share of these positions, than was warranted by their share of seats, as shown in the case of the UPA government of 2004 (Table 4.6).

In contrast to the coalitions at the centre, the coalitions at the state level have been more stable, characterized by a higher ideological compatibility, stable pre-electoral seat-sharing arrangements, as well as stable portfolio allocation when in power (Sridharan 2014: 459).

TABLE 4.6 Seat Share and Ministers of Smaller Parties in the UPA Government, 2004

Party	Seats in the Lok Sabha		Ministers		Cabinet Ministers	
	Number	Share	Number	Share	Number	Share
RJD	24	4.4%	8	11.9%	2	7.1%
DMK	16	2.9%	7	10.4%	3	10.7%
NCP	9	1.7%	3	4.5%	1	3.6%
PMK	6	1.1%	2	3.0%	1	3.6%
LJP	4	0.7%	1	1.5%	1	3.6%
Total	59	10.8%	21	31.3%	8	28.6%

Source: Rediff (2004).

A complex mix of sociological, institutional, and contextual factors created circumstances that were conducive to, and led to the fragmentation of the Indian party system in the late 1980s and the 1990s. The rise of identity politics, the effect of India's electoral system that facilitated alliances, the macro-context of the Congress's decline, and a clientelistic brand of politics contributed towards the emergence and growth of regional parties and the BJP. Over time, this has led to a new form of multiparty polity, whereby national and regional parties coexist, form alliances to enhance their electoral prospects, and share power at the national level and in the states.

This diffused political scenario led to and was shaped by the formation of coalition governments becoming a norm rather than the exception at the national level and in many states. The coalition governments at the centre have often comprised a large number of diverse 'office-seeking' rather than 'policy-seeking' parties, and were not able to last their full term until 1999. Thereafter, the coalition governments became more stable, having been led by the two major national parties, the Congress and the BJP. Regional parties have been pivotal to the formation and survival of the coalition governments formed at the national level during the period between 1989 and 2009, although they have often switched alliances and served in cabinets led by different political parties. The latest 2014 national election, however, marked a departure from this trend where the BJP, due to its majority in the Lok Sabha, is not dependent on the regional parties for the survival of the NDA coalition it leads.

The fragmentation of the Indian party system and the rise of regional parties also resulted in Indian states becoming the primary arenas of political contestation, a trend which has continued. Reflecting on this trend, Yadav and Palshikar (2009) argue that political choices in a national election continue to derive from the dynamics of state politics in the era of party fragmentation, which also provides opportunities for the regional parties to be influential at the national level. However, they caution that this primacy of the state level, which was facilitated by the democratic upsurge of the early 1990s, has also led to shrinking space for a real opposition. Similarly, Ziegfeld (2016: 253) argues that since the success of regional parties depends on a clientelistic brand of politics rather than their ability to represent subnational identities, their ineffectiveness in securing substantial devolution of power, even after having served in numerous national governments, is not surprising. Thus, the impact of fragmentation of the Indian party system and coalition governments on the Indian polity and democracy paints a mixed picture.

5

Emerging Trends in the Indian Party System

A key feature of the Indian party system today is the presence of a few national parties and a large number of regional parties that have presence only in one or few states. Further, the electoral base of national parties does not span the whole country and they often need to ally with regional parties to increase their chances of gaining power and forming governments at the centre. At the state level, too, the days of single-party dominance are largely over but the trend has varied across states, with the focus of the large parties having shifted to form intra- and inter-state electoral alliances to win the maximum number of seats.

Party System as It Stands Today

Based on the ECI's categorization, there were 6 national and 39 state parties that contested the 2014 general election, in which the BJP won a majority in the Lok Sabha. Due to the scale of the BJP's victory and the Congress's defeat, the 2014 national election was viewed as potentially being a critical or realigning election, which could signal the advent of a new phase of a BJP-dominant party system. More generally, this election challenged the assumption that the Indian party system was so fragmented that a single party could not achieve an outright majority.

The 2014 National Election

The BJP's campaign in the 2014 election was led by Narendra Modi, who had been the chief minister of Gujarat for over a decade, and was the party's prime ministerial candidate. Rahul Gandhi, Rajiv Gandhi's son, and Indira Gandhi's grandson, led the Congress campaign, and was its de facto prime ministerial candidate. The election results were significant in a number of ways. It was the first time since the 1984 election that a single party, the BJP, had won a majority (282 of 543) in the Lok Sabha after more than two decades of coalition and minority governments at the centre. The Congress, on the other hand, slipped to its lowest ever tally of 44 seats, and could not even claim the status of the main opposition party.

The positive swing towards the BJP was concentrated mainly in the Hindi belt and the states in the western region (Diwakar 2016a), and this called into question the claim that this election was transformational and was a move towards the nationalization of the Indian party system. Regional parties continued to dominate in many states. In West Bengal, the AITC under Mamata Banerjee's leadership won 34 of the 42 seats; the BJD led by Naveen Patnaik won 20 of the 21 seats in Odisha; while in Tamil Nadu, the AIADMK led by J. Jayalalithaa won 37 of the 39 seats. However, regional parties such as the BSP and SP in Uttar Pradesh and the RJD in Bihar, which had gained prominence in the 1990s by mobilizing around caste identities, failed to win a significant number of seats. The two main Left parties—the CPM and the CPI—which were crucial in the formation and survival of many previous coalitions at the centre, continued to face electoral decline, and in total, won only 10 seats (4 per cent vote share) compared to 20 (6.8 per cent vote share) in 2009 and 53 (7.1 per cent vote share) in 2004. These two parties face challenges in inducting fresh talent in their leadership ranks and attracting young voters in a significant manner.

The trend of decline in the vote and seat share of national parties versus the state and other parties continued in the 2014 national election. In 1989, national parties had won 89 per cent of the seats and 79 per cent of the votes but these shares dropped to 63 per cent and 61 per cent, respectively, in 2014. Although ENP by seats at the national level declined from 5.0 in 2009 to 3.5 in 2014 mainly due to the BJP gaining a seat majority, ENP by votes witnessed a smaller decline from 7.6 to 6.9 during this period. ENP by votes has averaged around 6.8 since the 1990s, and therefore, an ENP of 6.9 in 2014 does not signal a clear reversal of the trend of fragmentation of the Indian party system.

Since Modi's 2014 election campaign focused primarily on economic growth and development, it was suggested that this election may mark a reversal of political fragmentation along caste and regional lines, where issues rather than identity become more important for the voters. However, doubts were also expressed whether this election marked a longer term realignment of the party system. In particular, the BJP's 2014 victory was achieved on the basis of the lowest ever vote share (31 per cent) received by a party winning the majority of seats, helped by the mechanics of SMPS that enabled it to convert a 12 per cent increase in vote share from 2009 into a much larger 31 per cent increase in seat share. And, to this extent, the BJP's seat majority is tenuous. The disproportionality of election results was also reflected in the BSP not being able to win any seat despite receiving a non-trivial

4.1 per cent of the national vote share, while regional parties AIADMK and AITC won 37 and 34 seats on the basis of smaller vote shares of 3.3 per cent and 3.8 per cent, respectively. Thus, this election highlighted that success of parties under SMPS remains dependent on the geographical concentration of their support rather than the absolute vote share, which incentivizes them to seek seat-sharing arrangements to minimize wasted votes.

State Assembly Elections, 2014–17

BJP's win in the 2014 national election was followed by its success in the state assembly elections in Haryana and Maharashtra in October 2014 (Diwakar 2016a). It secured a majority in Haryana, and emerged as the single largest party in Maharashtra to form a coalition government. These victories were followed by BJP's better-than-expected performance in Jharkhand and Jammu and Kashmir state assembly elections in December 2014. In Jharkhand, it won the largest number of seats and led the formation of a coalition government. In Jammu and Kashmir, it won the largest share of votes but secured the second largest number of seats, and formed an unlikely post-poll coalition government with the PDP.

The BJP continued its strategy of leveraging Modi's popularity in the Delhi and Bihar state assembly elections held in February and October 2015, respectively. However, it was defeated by the AAP in Delhi and by a grand alliance (*Mahagathbandhan*) between the RJD, JDU, and Congress in Bihar. In Delhi, the AAP led by Arvind Kejriwal, won a historic victory winning 67 of the 70 seats based on an anti–corruption agenda (Diwakar 2016b). In Bihar, the BJP's loss was attributed to not projecting a chief ministerial candidate to take on the grand alliance's candidate—the JDU's Nitish Kumar. As Chakrabarty (2016: 19) states, 'Modi was unable to assuage Bihari voters who felt cheated by the BJP seeking to impose a bahari [outsider] as their chief minister'. Although the BJP received the highest (24.4 per cent) vote share, parties which were part of the grand alliance avoided fragmentation of their votes under SMPS and were able to win a majority of seats.

Assembly elections were held in the states of Assam, West Bengal, Tamil Nadu, and Kerala in May 2016. The BJP projected a local leader as its chief ministerial candidate in Assam, which was an important factor for its first ever win in a major state in the eastern part of the country. In West Bengal and Tamil Nadu assembly elections, the trends from the 2014 general election continued with victories by regional parties, the AITC and AIADMK, respectively. In Kerala, the

Left Democratic Front (LDF) won 91 seats, followed by the Congress-led United Democratic Front (UDF) at 47. The results of these elections showed that national and state assembly elections can produce different winning parties, even if these are held in quick succession. Political landscape remains complex, and as Chakrabarty (2016: 19) argues, 'it is simply impossible to conceive of a universal conceptual framework of analysis of elections in India'.

As this book went to press, results of the latest round of assembly elections in five states—Uttar Pradesh, Punjab, Goa, Uttarakhand, and Manipur—held during February–March 2017 were announced. The BJP swept the elections in Uttar Pradesh, the largest and the most important state electorally, Uttarakhand, and also succeeded in forming coalition governments in Manipur and Goa despite finishing second to the Congress in the number of seats. Punjab was the only state where the Congress emerged victorious, ending the decade-long tenure of the coalition government comprising the SAD and the BJP. The AAP finished a distant second in Punjab in respect of seats, could not win any seat in Goa, and its ambition to expand beyond Delhi suffered a setback.

In addition to being in power at the centre, the BJP now controls governments in states comprising more than 60 per cent of India's population, and is

131

well-positioned to implement its manifesto promises, including reforms and measures to facilitate rapid economic growth and development. Its unprecedented victory in Uttar Pradesh contrasted with the electoral losses suffered by the two prominent regional parties—the incumbent SP (that fought the election in alliance with the Congress) and the BSP—whose success since the 1990s was largely due to mobilization of the SC population. Their defeat could, therefore, potentially diminish incentives for parties to engage in clientelistic appeals to specific groups of voters. The BJP's performance in the latest state assembly elections has further strengthened Modi's position as the country's most visible leader, and confirms the conclusion that the BJP has replaced the Congress as the principal national party in India.

Indian Party System: A Prognosis

The Indian party system today includes the BJP as the principal national party, which is strong in the Hindi belt, western and northern parts of the country; the Congress, the other national party, which continues to face decline; and many regional parties that have concentrated bases of support in specific parts of the country. Despite the BJP's victory in the 2014 national election and in many subsequent state assembly elections, India remains a multiparty system, which is a complex summation of the state-level party systems, where national and regional parties compete as well as ally with each other. The party system remains in a state of flux, where parties continue to form, split, and merge, and the increase in the number of parties in the recent years is in contrast to the one-party dominant system that existed during the first two decades after Independence.

Further, the support base of the national parties no longer spans the whole country, and they have to often rely on alliances with regional parties to increase their chances of gaining power at the centre and in the states. The vote and the seat share of the regional parties has continued to increase, especially since the 1996 national election, while that of the national parties has declined. In many states, the regional parties are the dominant players while the national parties have limited presence.

These features have led to a multiparty system at the national level and diverse nature of party competition in different states. Some states have moved to a bipolar competition between regional or national parties, while in others the competition is multipolar between one or more national and regional parties. Different regional parties are influential in different parts of the country, while the support base of national parties has continued to shrink. The diversity of the state-level party systems also makes it difficult to generalize about the nature of the Indian party system, and makes the political situation volatile. These features of the Indian party system took shape especially in the 1980s and the 1990s, following the decline of the Congress and the fragmentation of the Indian party system, and in most part, continue to hold today.

Although the BJP has emerged as the principal national party in India, it is not as yet a 'system-defining' or a 'dominant' party, as the Congress was in the 1950s and the 1960s. The key difference is that there are many states, especially in the southern and the eastern parts of the country, where the BJP has not been successful due to the presence of influential regional parties. In the period of its dominance, the Congress represented a multitude of interests and had a pan-national appeal, and as a result, it was able to get support from a wide electoral base consisting of various social groups. The BJP, on the other hand, has to compete in a more competitive political environment, where there has been a politicization of numerous social cleavages, making it difficult for a party to build a broad-based national support base. Its growth is also restricted by a lack of support from Muslims, which comprise a significant proportion of the population in many states. It is also not yet the majority party in the Rajya Sabha, which impedes its ability to pass legislations, although based on the latest state assembly elections, it may also be able to gain control of the Rajya Sabha in the future.

The results of the 2015 Bihar state assembly election have shown that if BJP's opponents can unite and forge an alliance against it, the party could face a challenge to sustain its success in the future elections. According to Chandra et al. (2008: 683), the BJP's recent growth can be attributed to the gradual disappearance of all other Right-wing parties, decline of the Congress, and the support from the growing middle classes in India. Although the BJP under Modi's leadership appears to be focusing on promoting inclusive growth and development, concerns remain whether the party will return to a more radical Hindutva agenda in the future.

A trend which has continued is of the Congress's decline, and it seems unable to effectively challenge the BJP at the national level. Especially after 1989, the Congress has not been active in promoting a political strategy to attract specific social sections, and has almost become a catch-none party. Its unexpected victory in the 2004 national election was circumstantial rather than based on any specific political strategy or increase in its electoral base, and further, the party continues to be heavily reliant on the Gandhi–Nehru family for leadership. Palshikar (2015b) points out that the real reason for the Congress's decline lies in ceding the sociopolitical space to other parties, and its continued failure in this regard will lead to its demise. Hasan (2012: 226) argues that during the post-Indira years, the Congress moved away from 'ideological frameworks' as part of the global tendency among political parties in the era of globalization, while Bijukumar (2006: 260–3) concludes that the revival of the Congress is only possible through a policy of distributive justice.

The decline of the Congress is worrying because it still is the only national party with a left-of-centre political ideology, and has an important role to play both as an opposition to the BJP as well as a potential party of power. However, its organization remains centralized, dependent on the Nehru–Gandhi dynasty, and over time, the party's ability to carry out political activities and communication at the grass-roots level has diminished. The Congress needs to seriously consider extensive organizational reforms, and cultivation of leaders beyond the Nehru–Gandhi dynasty to recover from its existential crisis. The AAP is attempting to move into the political space vacated by the Congress but as things stand now, the emergence of an alternative political formation to Congress, as a broad-based umbrella party, looks unlikely.

There are no clear signs of improvement in the electoral prospects of the two principal Communist parties, the CPM and the CPI. This is also not a positive sign, since India needs diversity of political opinions and views to be represented through political parties, and in most part, these parties have been exceptions to the opportunistic brand of politics in India. However, in order to revive themselves, these parties need to review their organization structure and political strategies in light of the changed political and economic environment in India.

In the emerging political landscape, the main challenge to the BJP at the national level is likely to arise from a coalition of regional parties or a coalition of regional parties plus the Congress. Regional leaders such as Mamata Banerjee of the AITC and Nitish Kumar of the JDU could potentially lead an anti-BJP national alliance for the 2019 national election. Arvind Kejriwal also has ambitions to emerge as a national leader and expand the AAP as a national political force, but the party's relatively poor performance in the recent state assembly elections in Punjab and Goa have diminished these prospects. Similarly, prominent regional leaders of Uttar Pradesh—Mulayam Singh Yadav and his son Akhilesh Yadav of the SP, and Mayawati of the BSP—have suffered a major electoral setback in the 2017 state assembly election. Although non-Congress, non–BJP parties were able to come together to form national governments in 1977, 1989, and 1996, they could not present an alternative development agenda or vision, and failed to last their full term due to lack of cohesion, and personality clashes. These factors continue to inhibit the formation of an alternative 'third front' at the national level, and as things stand now, only the BJP and the Congress remain the likely parties to form or lead the governments at the centre.

Coalition Politics

Table 5.1 shows that given the trend of seats won by the top two and other parties, it will be challenging for the BJP to repeat its 2014 electoral performance and achieve a majority of seats in the Lok Sabha, even if it remains the principal national party in India. Column A of Table 5.1 shows that before the 1989 election, parties other than the top two won around 100 seats (averaging 119) in the Lok Sabha. However, in the subsequent elections, this number saw a dramatic increase, almost doubling to an average of 221. Thus, in order to win a majority, a party now needs to have a lead of more than 200 seats over the runner-up party—Column E of Table 5.1. This level of lead has only happened once (in 2014 election) in the last eight elections held during the period of 1989–2014, while the actual average lead of the top party over the second-ranked party has only been 79 seats (Column F of Table 5.1).

TABLE 5.1 Lead Required to Win a Majority in Lok Sabha, 1952–2014

Election	Actual Seats Won by Parties Other than the Top Two	Actual Seats Won by Top Two Parties	Seats Required to Win a Majority[1]	Seats Left for Runner-up Party[2]	Lead Required by Top Party Over Runner-up Party to Secure a Majority[3]	Actual Lead of Top Party Over Runner-up Party[4]	Total Seats
	(A)	(B)	(C)	(D)	(E)	(F)	(G)
1952	109	380	246	134	112	348	489
1957	96	398	248	150	98	344	494
1962	104	390	248	142	106	332	494
1967	193	327	261	66	195	239	520
1971	141	377	260	117	143	327	518
1977	93	449	272	177	95	141	542
1980	135	394	266	128	138	312	529
1984	80	434	258	176	82	374	514
1989	189	340	266	74	192	54	529
1991	169	352	262	90	172	112	521

(Contd.)

Table 5.1 (*Contd.*)

	(A)	(B)	(C)	(D)	(E)	(F)	(G)
1996	242	301	273	28	245	21	543
1998	220	323	273	50	223	41	543
1999	247	296	273	23	250	68	543
2004	260	283	273	10	263	7	543
2009	221	322	273	49	224	90	543
2014	217	326	273	53	220	238	543
Average 1952–84	119	394			121	302	
Average 1989–2014	221	318			223	79	
Average 1952–2014	170	356			172	191	

Source: Author's calculations based on ECI election statistics.

Notes: 1. Majority = 50 per cent of total seats plus 1; 2. Seats won by top two party less majority mark (Column B less Column C); 3. Seats required to win a majority less won by runner-up party (Column C less Column D); and 4. Actual lead based on election results.

Further, the BJP's 2014 victory rested heavily on its dramatic success to convert votes into seats under SMPS, and its seat majority can be eroded even with a small negative swing in its vote share. In summary, the phenomenon of a single party having achieved a majority in 2014 might not be repeated in the near future even if a party manages to emerge as the single largest party in Lok Sabha. This, in turn, will entail the continued importance of parties entering into pre-poll and post-poll alliances, and the relevance of coalition politics in India.

It is also important to note that in the 2014 national election, the BJP won 57 of its 282 seats in states where it had electoral alliances with other parties. Since the party does not yet have a majority in the Rajya Sabha, it needs to engage with regional parties to facilitate passage of legislation. For the Congress, forging electoral alliances is of even greater importance, which was evident in its decision to enter in an alliance with regional parties in the 2015 Bihar state assembly election as a junior alliance partner, and to fight the 2016 West Bengal state election against the AITC, in an alliance with the CPM. The Congress also contested the 2017 Uttar Pradesh state assembly election as a junior alliance partner to the SP. Coalition politics is likely to remain important also because national and regional parties often need to form alliances to win elections at the state level, especially since Indian states remain important areas of political activity and mobilization for parties.

The decentralization of political and economic power to the states (Chhibber and Kollman 2004; Diwakar 2010) and a separate timetable for the Lok Sabha and state assembly elections (Tillin 2015) continue to offer substantial opportunities for the regional parties to be influential, especially in the state assembly elections. According to Farooqui and Sridharan (2014), under SMPS, the formation of alliances with parties helps aggregate constituency-level vote shares in states where one's own party is not strong enough to contest alone. Similarly, Palshikar et al. (2014) conclude that the 'normalization' of multiparty and coalition politics means that post-Congress polity will remain multiparty, and will be sustained through coalitions, although these may not be permanent thus retaining some instability and unpredictability in the electoral outcomes.

Importance of Political Leadership

Modi's success and campaigning style in the 2014 national election highlighted the growing importance of political leadership in mobilizing voters and winning elections in the Indian situation. For example,

Sridharan (2014: 28) notes that 'half the CSDS [Centre for the Study of Developing Societies] survey's respondents said leadership was important, and as many as a quarter of NDA voters told the CSDS post-election survey that had the [NDA] alliance not put Modi forward as its candidate for the premiership, they would not have cast their ballots for it'. That said, the importance of Modi's leadership in the 2014 national election needs to be understood within the context of the leadership presented by the candidates of rival parties. As Jaffrelot and Verniers (2015: 41) argue, 'the voters were certainly asking for more political authority after 10 years of a rather self-effacing prime minister [Dr. Manmohan Singh]'.

Chhibber and Ostermann (2014) point out that according to academic studies based on Western democracies, leaders of parties that have a clear ideological base are not expected to make a significant difference to electoral outcomes, and to this extent, Modi's impact on the 2014 national election was unexpected. Political leadership, however, assumes greater significance in the Indian context since parties have largely converged on major policy matters, and differentiate themselves mainly on the basis of leadership styles and performance (Palshikar et al. 2014). The advent of social media has also facilitated the trend of growing importance of leaders who communicate directly with voters on behalf of their parties, which has also been termed as the 'presidentialization' of parliamentary politics. The emergence of the AAP and its success in the 2015 Delhi state assembly election was largely attributed to the leadership provided by Arvind Kejriwal who effectively used the issue of corruption for political mobilization (Wyatt 2015). Gradual centralization of power in the hands of the heads of national and state governments in India have made them the centre of party mobilization strategies, which further emphasizes the importance of political leadership in sustaining the success of parties.

Over five decades ago, Sirsikar (1965: 522) had stated,

> Leadership based on the tradition of sacrifice, dedication and austerity would be replaced by the new leaders who represent their hold on their regions, either due to caste or interest group support....The role and influence of the state Chief Ministers will be more significant in years to come. This might be regarded as a consequence of the strength of regionalism.

This prediction has come true for the rise of regional parties, many of which are led by charismatic leaders, who are also the main campaigners for their party. However, the centralized nature of functioning of these 'single-leader parties' is not much different from that of dynastic parties, and can prevent induction of fresh talent, and discourage free dissent and debate within the party. Many recent state assembly elections, for example, Bihar and Assam, have shown that having strong regional leaders is important for national parties, and there are limitations to the influence of national leaders in state assembly elections. Modi's ascent from chief minister of a state to the country's prime minister is another evidence of the importance of grooming regional leaders to assume leadership roles at the national level. However, the importance of regional leadership remains election- and context-specific; the BJP's major victory in the recent 2017 Uttar Pradesh state assembly election was achieved on the basis of Modi's appeal as a national leader instead of the party's reliance on projecting a local chief ministerial candidate.

The growing control of charismatic leaders over their parties in the Indian context also presents a risk of control of party resources by few elites, akin to Robert Michels's formulation of the 'Iron Law of Oligarchy'. According to Michels (1962), due to division of labour, hierarchy, and control, decision-making and resources in large and complex organizations become centralized in the hands of a few elites, and this 'oligarchic rule' is sustained by leaders through manipulation, oratory, persuasion, and reward distribution. In the Indian context, this tendency is also subject to various pulls and pressures, including caste and regional affiliations of leaders. One of the strengths of many regional parties has been their charismatic leaders, but unless these parties develop a second rung of leaders, this factor can also become a major weakness. In the Indian context, the loyalty of party members is often towards the leader rather than to the ideological principles of the party. The political infighting and leadership crisis in the AIADMK following the demise of their leader J. Jayalalithaa in December 2016 illustrates this issue. However, given the multidimensional nature of political leadership in India, which is based on individual traits, as well as identity such as belonging to a dynasty or a specific caste, there are limitations to drawing any linear generalizations about the importance of the contextual factor of leadership in shaping parties and party systems (Diwakar 2016a).

Relevance of Identity Politics

Palshikar et al. (2014: 22) argue that a major change during 2002–12 has been the reduction of the political salience of the cleavages of religion and caste, and that 'it would be difficult for cleavage politics to shape at the all-India level in the contemporary circumstances'.

The nature of the BJP's campaign and success in the 2014 election as well as the relatively poor performance of parties such as the BSP, SP, and RJD also suggested that India may move from the politics of identity and clientelism towards issue- and ideology-based party politics. However, caste and more generally, identity is likely to remain an important, if not a decisive, electoral factor in the future. This was evidenced in the 2015 Bihar state assembly election, where a combination of caste and regional identity proved crucial in ensuring the victory of the grand alliance against the BJP, which focused mainly on the issues of economic growth and development. Although identity is likely to remain an important political factor in the Indian context, the results of the 2014 national election and the recent 2017 Uttar Pradesh state assembly election indicate that this factor alone may not be sufficient for parties to win elections.

While the BJP's victory in the 2014 national and many subsequent state assembly elections have provided it with a platform to realign Indian politics and the party system, its ability to do so will depend on whether the party can further expand its support base. Further, if Modi fails to deliver on his electoral promises, the BJP could lose support especially given the anti-incumbency bias usually faced by governments in India, and its tenuous majority under SMPS. For the Congress, electoral losses have continued, and its status and future as a national party is at risk. However, it could still make a comeback, as it has been able to do, for example in 1980 and 1991. There has been a role reversal between the Congress and the BJP in the last 10 to 15 years. Like the BJP in the past, the Congress today does not have a national presence. The BJP, on the other hand, has grown in its influence in regions where it did not have much presence in the past, and appears to be stronger than any national party since the Congress in 1984 (Diwakar 2016a).

Caste and region remain important election issues and regional parties continue to be strong in many parts of the country. It is still premature to view the 2014 election as a critical election in respect of the BJP becoming a system-defining party, and the end of coalition politics in India, even though the BJP has replaced the Congress as the country's principal national party. The large disproportionality between votes and seats seen in recent elections highlight the limitations of SMPS in India amidst a fragmented party system, and given India's diffused political environment, achieving a legislative majority at the national level remains a difficult proposition for a single party. Although AAP's performance in the 2017 state assembly elections in Punjab and Goa was below par, and its national ambition has suffered a setback, it still leads the state government in Delhi, is the main opposition party in Punjab, and thus remains a challenge for the more established parties, particularly the Congress. It is unclear whether and to what extent the AAP will be able to sustain its success in the state of Delhi and grow in other states, but its entry into the political arena has illustrated that with a well-thought-out electoral strategy, a credible leader, and an innovative communication strategy, the traditional high barriers to entry in Indian politics can be overcome.

The recently concluded 2017 state assembly elections, particularly in Uttar Pradesh, have further strengthened the BJP's central position in the Indian political scene. According to Dunleavy (2010), a dominant political party is able to deny a significant section of the ideological spectrum to any other rival party, even if the level of its success fluctuates depending on its own policy choices and the strategies adopted by the opposition parties and the level of coordination amongst them. The BJP under Modi's leadership has attempted to build its electoral strategy based on a combination of an all-India political narrative and state-specific factors, and its success in Uttar Pradesh will encourage it to continue to do so in future elections to counter the regional parties and the Congress.

As things stand now, the BJP appears to be succeeding in dominating the ideological space by straddling between an agenda based on inclusive development for all sections of the society, and using religious appeals to consolidate the Hindu vote in its favour. Although it is too early to judge how sustainable this two-pronged electoral strategy will be in the future, Modi remains the country's most powerful politician with no other leader capable of matching his national stature. It also appears unlikely that a single party will be able to dislodge Modi in the 2019 national election, and the emergence of a credible anti-BJP coalition of the regional parties with or without the Congress also remains improbable. The BJP is, therefore, poised to maintain its status as the principal national party, and is also at the threshold of becoming a system-defining or dominant political party in India.

In a significant recent development, Nitish Kumar of the JDU resigned as Bihar's chief minister in July 2017, following allegations of corruption against one of the leaders of the RJD, the other main party in the coalition government. In a dramatic move, the JDU and the BJP decided to form a new coalition government in Bihar, with Nitish Kumar returning as the chief minister. This has further strengthened the BJP's position to the detriment of the RJD and the Congress, which were part of the previous coalition government in Bihar. This development has further diminished the possibility of a strong opposition front to challenge the BJP in the 2019 national election.

Conclusion

India currently has a multiparty system, which allows for the representation of diverse views and opinions. Parties form a part of an evolving party system both at the national and the state levels, and they remain central to the sustenance of India's democratic politics and culture. Indian democracy has remained relatively stable, in which parties have used constitutional means in the form of elections to fight political and ideological battles leading to peaceful transfer of power between governments. However, to continue to fulfil their role effectively, parties in India face many challenges and issues, including criminality in politics, use of money and muscle power in elections, developing effective organizations and leaders, and ensuring internal democracy.

About one-third of the members of parliament (MPs) of the current (16th) Lok Sabha have criminal charges filed against them (ADR 2016). Although the Supreme Court of India has ruled that convicted MPs and state legislative assemblies will be disqualified from their membership, delays inherent in the Indian judicial process remains a key hurdle to address this issue. The use of money and muscle power to allocate seats and win elections is routinely highlighted by press reports, and this has led to calls for parties to become more transparent about their sources of funding. Gowda and Sridharan (2012) argue that India's complex election expenditure, funding, and disclosure laws foster the reliance of parties on unaccounted funds for contesting elections, and suggest some possible remedies, including partial state funding of political parties, to help address this unhealthy situation. Some recent steps to address this problem include a measure in the 2017–18 union budget to reduce maximum cash donations to a political party, and the demonetization or banning of high-denomination notes to reduce unaccounted money in the economy. Prime Minister Modi has also brought to the forefront an idea to hold concurrent national and state assembly elections to reduce the costs of conducting and fighting elections, an idea that is worthy of debate.

Most parties in India have become primarily an instrument of power, and tend to have a short-term outlook driven by immediate electoral gains rather than a long-term political or development vision. This, in turn, has led to parties adopting clientelistic promises of providing free goods and services, and relying mainly on 'identity politics' of appealing to voters based on caste, religion, or region. Wilkinson (2015) observes that India appears to have a strong democracy without strong parties or a stable party system because Indian parties are still very clientelistic, and to that extent the definition of party weakness has to be re-evaluated. However, India's clientelistic style of politics is far from ideal since it goes hand in hand with corruption, redistributes inefficiently, and rarely puts pressure on politicians to provide comprehensive, long-term solutions to the country's ills (Ziegfeld 2016: 254). Wyatt (2013) makes the point that parties within a clientelist political system may still decide to dilute their clientelist strategies by the addition of programmatic policies to appeal to voters.

Although the Supreme Court of India has recently held that religion, race, caste, community, or language would not be allowed to play any role in the electoral process, it is difficult to assess how this ruling will be implemented in practice in light of the very existence of many parties being based on supporting specific castes and social groups. As Khilnani (2003: 58) argues, although regional and caste politics, and Hindu nationalism embody different potentialities, they are direct products of India's first four decades of Independence, and it is wrong to see them as atavistic forms that attack the ideas of the state and democracy; 'on the contrary, they exemplify the triumphant success of these ideas'.

Many parties also suffer from the issue of extreme personalization, placing their leaders or a dynasty above the party, thus hindering the emergence of new leaders. This can weaken the party organization and destabilize the party system. Almost 30 per cent of the MPs in the fifteenth Lok Sabha (following the 2009 election) were nominated for election by virtue of their family networks in politics (French 2010). Similarly, Chandra (2016a) finds that between 2004 and 2014 about a quarter of the MPs in the Lok Sabha, on an average, have had a dynastic background. According to Chhibber (2013), the presence of dynastic parties has negative consequences in respect of making the party system more unstable and the political system less representative. However, Chandra (2016b) argues that dynastic politics has also had an inclusive effect by providing a channel for representation for members of certain social categories—women, backward castes,

Muslims, and youth—who would not have otherwise found a space in politics.

Another negative feature of the Indian party system which has emerged in the last two decades is extreme opportunistic politics, where parties and leaders change alliances only to gain power rather than based on ideological congruence. Public trust in parties remains one of the lowest compared to other public institutions and Indian democracy in general, which discourages talented and idealistic individuals to enter politics. As Chandra et al. (2008: 681) point out, 'Political parties, which are the kingpins of a democratic political structure, have gradually become the weakest link in India's political system'.

A competitive party system should allow for new parties to form and participate in the democratic process. However, smaller and new parties in India face high barriers to entry and expansion in the political space due to the twin pressures of the mechanics of SMPS and the need to fund elections that have become increasingly costly. This calls for a more focused debate on reforming the electoral rules, as well as robust measures to govern electoral funding for parties, and keep criminals out of mainstream politics.

Despite all the challenges faced by the parties in India, they remain the most important link between the state and its citizens. Strong political parties and a competitive party system remain central to the functioning of a complex and diverse Indian democracy, and without them, the country could move towards an authoritarian brand of politics.

On their part, parties need to make their decision-making processes more democratic and sources of funding more transparent, and adopt a longer term political agenda instead of focusing exclusively on winning the next election at any cost. How well Indian political parties rise to the challenge of effectively representing India's diverse electorate and fulfilling their growing aspirations will be instrumental in India becoming a more liberal and stronger democracy in the future. Seventy years after Independence, a vibrant and competitive party system remains key to the Indian political life, and the role of political parties in the survival and functioning of Indian democracy remains paramount.

References

ADR (Association of Democratic Reforms). 2016. Available at http://myneta.info/search_myneta.php?q=criminal+charges, accessed on 12 July 2017.

Arora, B., K.K. Kailash, Rekha Saxena, and H. Kham Khan Suan. 2013. 'Indian Federalism', in K.C. Suri and A. Vanaik (eds), *Political Science*, vol. 2, *Indian Democracy*, pp. 101–61. New Delhi: Oxford University Press.

Aldrich, J. 1995. *Why Parties? The Origin and the Transformation of Party Politics in America*. Chicago: University of Chicago Press.

Bose, A. 2009. 'Hindutva and the Politicisation of the Religious Identity in India', *Journal of Peace, Conflict and Development*, 13 (February): 1–30.

Bijukumar, V. 2006. *Reinventing the Congress*. Jaipur: Rawat Books.

Chakrabarty, B. 2014. *Coalition Politics in India*. New Delhi: Oxford University Press.

———. 2016. 'Defying the Pattern: The 2016 State Assembly Elections', *Economic and Political Weekly*, 51 (43): 18–20.

Chandra, B., M. Mukherjee, and A. Mukherjee. 2008. *India since Independence*. New Delhi: Penguin Books.

Chandra, K. 2004. *Why Ethnic Parties Succeed: Patronage and Ethnic Head Counts in India*. New York: Cambridge University Press.

——— (ed.). 2016a. 'Prologue', in *Democratic Dynasties: State, Party and Family in Contemporary Indian Politics*, pp. 1–11. Cambridge: Cambridge University Press.

——— (ed.). 2016b. 'Democratic Dynasties', in *Democratic Dynasties*, pp. 12–55. Cambridge: Cambridge University Press.

Chhibber, P.K. 2013. 'Dynastic Parties: Organization, Finance and Impact', *Party Politics*, 19 (2): 277–95.

Chhibber, P.K. and G. Murali. 2006. 'Duvergerian Dynamics in the Indian States', *Party Politics*, 12 (1): 5–34.

Chhibber, P.K. and I. Nooruddin. 2004. 'Do Party Systems Count? The Number of Parties and Government Performance in Indian States', *Comparative Political Studies*, 37 (2): 152–87.

Chhibber, P.K. and J. Petrocik. 1989. 'The Puzzle of Indian Politics: Social Cleavages and the Indian Party System', *British Journal of Political Science*, 19 (2): 191–210.

Chhibber, P.K. and K. Kollman. 2004. *The Formation of National Party Systems: Federalism and Party Competition in Britain, Canada, India*. Princeton: Princeton University Press.

Chhibber P.K. and S.L. Ostermann. 2014. 'The BJP's Fragile Mandate: Modi and Vote Mobilisers in the 2014 General Elections', *Studies in Indian Politics*, 2 (2): 137–51.

Cox, G. 1997. *Making Votes Count: Strategic Coordination in the World's Electoral Systems*. Cambridge: Cambridge University Press.

Desai, M. 2009. *The Rediscovery of India*. New Delhi: Penguin Books.

Diwakar, R. 2007. 'Duverger's Law and the Size of the Indian Party System', *Party Politics*, 13 (5): 539–61.

—————. 2010. 'Party Aggregation in India: A State Level Analysis', *Party Politics*, 16 (4): 477–96.

—————. 2011. 'Political Parties', in K. Dowding (ed.), *Encyclopedia of Power*, pp. 492–4. Thousand Oaks: SAGE Publications.

—————. 2016a. 'Change and Continuity in Indian Politics and the Indian Party System', *Asian Journal of Comparative Politics*, pp. 1–20, doi: 10.1177/2057891116679309.

—————. 2016b. 'Local Contest, National Impact: Understanding the Success of India's Aam Aadmi Party in 2015 Delhi Assembly Election', *Representation*, 52 (1): 71–80.

Dunleavy, P. 2010. 'Rethinking Dominant Party Systems', in M. Bogaards and F. Boucek (eds), *Dominant Political Parties and Democracy*, pp. 23–44. London: Routledge.

Duverger, M. 1963 [1954]. *Political Parties: Their Organization and Activity in the Modern State*. New York: John Wiley and Sons.

Farooqui, A. and E. Sridharan. 2014. 'Is the Coalition Era Over in Indian Politics?' *The Round Table: Commonwealth Journal of International Affairs*, 103 (6): 1–13.

French, P. 2010. *India: A Portrait, An Intimate Biography of 1.2 Billion People*. UK: Allen Lane/ Penguin.

Gowda, M.V.R. and E. Sridharan. 2012. 'Reforming India's Party Financing and Election Expenditure Laws', *Election Law Journal*, 11 (2): 226–40.

Graham, B.D. 1987. 'The Jana Sangh and Bloc Politics, 1967–80', *The Journal of Commonwealth and Comparative Politics*, 25 (3): 248–66.

——. 2006. 'The Challenge of Hindu Nationalism: The Bharatiya Janata Party in Contemporary Indian Politics', in P.R. DeSouza and E. Sridharan (eds), *India's Political Parties*, pp. 155–72. New Delhi: SAGE Publications.

Grofman, B., A. Chiaramonte, R. D'Alimonte, and S.L. Feld. 2004. 'Comparing and Contrasting the Uses for Two Graphical Tools for Displaying Patterns of Multiparty Competition: Nagayama Diagrams and Simplex Representations', *Party Politics*, 10 (3): 273–99.

Guha, R. 2007. *India after Gandhi: The History of the World's Largest Democracy*. London: MacMillan.

Gunther, R. and L. Diamond. 2001. 'Types and Functions of Parties', in L. Diamond and R. Gunther (eds), *Political Parties and Democracy*, pp. 3–39. Baltimore: Johns Hopkins University Press.

Hasan, Z. 2012. *Congress After Indira: Policy, Power, Political Change (1984–2009)*. New Delhi: Oxford University Press.

Hewitt, V. 2008. *Political Mobilization and Democracy in India: States of Emergency*. New York: Routledge.

Hindmoor, A. 2006. *Rational Choice*. New York: Palgrave Macmillan.

Jaffrelot, C. (ed.). 2010. *Religion, Caste and Politics in India*. Delhi: Primus Books.

——. 2013. 'Refining the Moderation Thesis. Two Religious Parties and Indian Democracy: The Jana Sangh and the BJP between Hindutva Radicalism and Coalition Politics', *Democratization*, 20 (5): 867–94.

Jaffrelot, C. and G. Verniers. 2015. 'The Resistance of Regionalism: BJP's Limitations and the Resilience of State Parties', in P. Wallace (eds), *India's 2014 Elections*, pp. 28–45. New Delhi. SAGE Publications.

Kailash, K.K. 2014a. 'Regional Parties in the 16th Lok Sabha Elections: Who Survived and Why?' *Economic and Political Weekly*, 49 (39): 64–71.

————. 2014b. 'Institutionalizing a Coalitional System and Games within Coalitions in India (1996–2014)', *Studies in Indian Politics*, 2 (2): 185–202.

Key, Jr. V.O. 1964. *Politics, Parties and Pressure Groups*, 5th edition. New York: Crowell.

Khilnani, S. 2003. *The Idea of India*. New Delhi: Penguin Books.

Kothari, R. 1964. 'The Congress "System" in India', *Asian Survey*, 4 (12): 1161–73.

————. 1970. *Politics in India*. Delhi: Sangam.

Laakso, M. and R. Taagepera. 1979. 'The "Effective" Number of Parties: A Measure with Application to West Europe', *Comparative Political Studies*, 12 (1): 3–27.

Lijphart, A. 1996. 'The Puzzle of Indian Democracy: A Consociational Interpretation', *The American Political Science Review*, 90 (2): 258–68.

Lipset, S.M. and S. Rokkan (eds). 1967. 'Cleavage Structures, Party Systems, and Voter Alignments: An Introduction', in *Party Systems and Voter Alignments: Cross-National Perspectives*, pp. 1–64. New York: Free Press.

Mehra, A.K. 2003. 'Introduction', in A.K. Mehra, D. Das Khanna, and G.W. Kueck (eds), *Political Parties and Party Systems*, pp. 21–48. New Delhi. SAGE Publications.

Mehra, A.K. 2013. *Party System in India: Emerging Trajectories*. New Delhi: Lancer Publishers.

Metcalf, B.D. and T.R. Metcalf. 2006. *A Concise History of Modern India*. Cambridge: Cambridge University Press.

Michels, R. 1962. *Political Parties: A Sociological Study of the Oligarchical Tendencies of Modern Democracy*. New York: Collier Books.

Morris-Jones, W.H. 1966. 'Dominance and Dissent: The Inter-relations in the Indian Party System', *Government and Opposition*, 1 (4): 451–66.

Nag, K. 2014. *The Saffron Tide*. New Delhi: Rupa Publications.

Neto, A.O. and G. Cox. 1997. 'Electoral Institutions, Cleavage Structures, and the Number of Parties', *American Journal of Political Science*, 41 (1): 149–74.

Pai, S. 1996. 'The Transformation of the Indian Party System', *Asian Survey*, 36 (12): 1170–83.

—————. 1998. 'The Indian Party System under Trans-formation: Lok Sabha Elections 1998', *Asian Survey*, 38 (9): 836–52.

Palshikar, S. 2003. 'The Regional Parties and Democracy: Romantic Rendezvous or Localised Legitimation', in A.K. Mehra, D.D. Khanna, and Gert W. Kueck (eds), *Political Parties and Party Systems*, pp. 306–35. New Delhi. SAGE Publications.

—————. 2012. 'Regional and Caste Parties', in A. Kohli and P. Singh (eds), *Routledge Handbook of Indian Politics*, pp. 91–104. Abingdon: Routledge.

—————. 2015a. 'The BJP and Hindu Nationalism: Centrist Politics and Majoritarian Impulses', *South Asia: Journal of South Asian Studies*, 38 (4): 719–35.

—————. 2015b. 'Congress in the Times of Post-Congress Era', *Economic and Political Weekly*, 50 (19): 39–46.

Palshikar, S., K.C. Suri, and Y. Yadav (eds). 2014. 'Introduction: Normalization of the "Post-Congress" Polity', in *Party Competition in Indian States: Electoral Politics in Post-Congress Polity*, pp. 1–42. New Delhi: Oxford University Press.

Rediff. 2004. 'Manmohan Singh, 67 Ministers Sworn In', 22 May, available at http://www.rediff.com/election/2004/may/22man.htm (accessed on 30 January 2017).

Riker, W. 1982. 'The Two-party System and Duverger's Law', *American Political Science Review*, 76 (4): 753–66.

Saez, L. and A. Sinha. 2010. 'Political Cycles, Political Institutions and Public Expenditure in India, 1980–2000', *British Journal of Political Science*, 40 (1): 91–113.

Sartori, G. 1976. *Parties and Party Systems*. Cambridge: Cambridge University Press.

Schakel, A.H. and W. Swenden. 2016. 'Rethinking Party System Nationalization in India (1952–2014)', *Government and Opposition*, pp. 1–25, doi:10.1017/gov.2015.42.

Sirsikar, V.M. 1965. 'Political Leadership in India', *Economic and Political Weekly*, 17 (12): 517–22.

Seshia, S. 1998. 'Divide and Rule in Indian Party Politics: The Rise of the Bharatiya Janata Party', *Asian Survey*, 38 (11): 1036–50.

Sridharan, E. 1997. 'Duverger's Law and Its Reformulations and the Evolution of the Indian Party System', IRIS India Working Paper. Maryland: University of Maryland.

—————. 2002. 'The Fragmentation of the Indian Party System, 1952–1999', in Z. Hasan (ed.), *Parties and*

Party Politics in India, pp. 475–503. New Delhi: Oxford University Press.

————. 2003. 'Coalitions and Party Strategies in India's Parliamentary Federation', *Publius: The Journal of Federalism*, 33 (4): 135–52.

————. 2005. 'Coalition Strategies and the BJP's Expansion, 1989–2004', *Commonwealth and Comparative Politics*, 43 (2): 194–221.

————. (ed.). 2014. 'National and State Coalitions in India: Theory and Comparison', in *Coalition Politics in India*, pp. 23–34. New Delhi: Academic Foundation.

Sridharan, E. and A. Varshney. 2001. 'Towards Moderate Pluralism: Political Parties in India', in L. Diamond and R. Gunther (eds), *Political Parties and Democracy*, pp. 206–37. Baltimore: The Johns Hopkins University Press.

Sridharan, E. and P.R. DeSouza. 2006. 'Introduction: The Evolution of Political Parties in India', in P.R. DeSouza and E. Sridharan (eds), *India's Political Parties*, pp. 15–36. New Delhi: SAGE Publications.

Suri, K.C. 2005. *Parties under Pressure: Political Parties in India since Independence*, project on State of Democracy in South Asia. New Delhi: Lokniti, Centre for the Study of Developing Societies.

Taagepera, R. and M. Shugart. 1989. *Seats and Votes: The Effects and Determinants of Electoral Systems*. New Haven: Yale University Press.

Thachil, T. 2014. *Elite Parties, Poor Voters*. Cambridge: Cambridge University Press.

Thachil, T. and E. Teitelbaum. 2015. 'Ethnic Parties and Public Spending: New Theory and Evidence from the Indian States', *Comparative Political Studies*, 48 (11): 1389–420.

Tillin, L. 2015. 'Regional Resilience and National Party System Change: India's 2014 General Elections in Context', *Contemporary South Asia*, 23 (2): 181–97.

Tudor, M. 2013. *The Promise of Power: The Origins of Democracy in India and Autocracy in Pakistan*. New Delhi: Cambridge University Press.

Varshney, A. 1993. 'Contested Meanings: India's National Identity, Hindu Nationalism, and the Politics of Anxiety', Daedalus, 122 (3): 227–61.

―――――. 2013. 'How Has Indian Federalism Done?' *Studies in Indian Politics*, 1 (1): 43–63.

Weiner, M. 2006. 'Party Politics and Electoral Behaviour: From Independence to the 1980s', in P.R. DeSouza and E. Sridharan (eds), *India's Political Parties*, pp. 73–115. New Delhi: SAGE Publications.

Wilkinson, S.I. 2007. 'Explaining Changing Patterns of Party-Voter Linkages in India', in H. Kitschelt and S.I. Wilkinson (eds), *Patrons, Clients and Policies: Patterns of Democratic Accountability and Political Competition*, pp. 110–40. Cambridge: Cambridge University Press.

―――――. 2015. 'Where's the Party? The Decline of Party Institutionalisation and What (If Anything) That Means for Democracy', *Government and Opposition*, 50 (3): 420–45.

Wyatt, A. 2009. *Party System Change in South India*. Abingdon: Routledge.

―――――. 2013. 'Combining Clientelist and Programmatic Politics in Tamil Nadu, South India', *Commonwealth and Comparative Politics*, 51 (1): 27–55.

―――――. 2015. 'Arvind Kejriwal's Leadership of the Aam Aadmi Party', *Contemporary South Asia*, 23 (2): 167–80.

Yadav, Y. 1996. 'Reconfiguration in Indian Politics: State Assembly Elections, 1993–95', *Economic and Political Weekly*, 31 (2/3): 95–104.

—————. 1999. Electoral Politics in the Time of Change: India's Third Electoral System, 1989–99', *Economic and Political Weekly*, 34 (34/35): 2393–9.

Yadav, Y. and S. Palshikar. 2006. 'Party System and Electoral Politics in the Indian States, 1952–2002: From Hegemony to Convergence', in P.R. DeSouza and E. Sridharan (eds), *India's Political Parties*, pp. 73–115. New Delhi: SAGE Publications.

—————. 2009. 'Principle State Level Contests and Derivative National Choices: Electoral Trends in 2004–9', *Economic and Political Weekly*, 44 (6): 55–62.

Ziegfeld, A. 2012. 'Coalition Government and Party System Change', *Comparative Politics*, 45 (1): 69–87.

—————. 2016. *Why Regional Parties? Clientelism, Elites, and the Indian Party System*. Cambridge: Cambridge University Press.

Websites

Communist Party of India: Available at http://www.communistparty.in/.

Election Commission of India, various years, election results, full statistical reports: http://eci.nic.in/eci_main1/ElectionStatistics.aspx.

Index

About the Author

REKHA DIWAKAR is a lecturer in politics at the University of Sussex, UK, since 2013. She is also a research associate at the London School of Economics and Political Science, UK. She has previously been a lecturer in politics and research methods at Goldsmiths, University of London, UK. Her research interests include Indian politics and public policy; comparative politics, especially electoral competition and voting behaviour; size of the party systems; and research methods in political science. Her works have been published in various well-known international journals and publications.